He Is Your Husband

He Is Your Husband

"I KNOW YOU ARE MY WIFE"

LINDA JOHNSON

WestBow
PRESS
A DIVISION OF THOMAS NELSON

WestBow Press books may be ordered through booksellers or by contacting:

WestBow Press
A Division of Thomas Nelson
1663 Liberty Drive
Bloomington, IN 47403
www.westbowpress.com
1-(866) 928-1240

Because of the dynamic nature of the Internet, any web addresses or links contained in this book may have changed since publication and may no longer be valid. The views expressed in this work are solely those of the author and do not necessarily reflect the views of the publisher, and the publisher hereby disclaims any responsibility for them.

Certain stock imagery © Thinkstock.
Any people depicted in stock imagery provided by Thinkstock are models, and such images are being used for illustrative purposes only.

ISBN: 978-1-4497-2032-2 (sc)

Library of Congress Control Number: 2011932555

Printed in the United States of America

WestBow Press rev. date: 6/30/2011

DEDICATION

To **Robert**, the military aviation combat pilot, which I met on Stemmons Freeway, in Dallas, Texas, in September 1995.

EPIGRAPH

"I am not to be compared, measured, explored,
exploited, nor dissected by a man. I am chosen, anointed,
prepared, and appointed by God to be a help meet,
to emanate into a functioning effective wife."

CONTENTS

INTRODUCTION

I was born, raised and currently live, in Dallas, Texas. Many of my weekends were spent in Gary, Texas, Panola County, which is my father Israel McCoy Johnson hometown, whereas, he was born and raised. My family enjoyed the sights of California each summer vacation, which is where my father's brothers and sisters live. Likewise, three of my mother's sisters relocated to California so later our summer vacations were split between Santa Maria, California, Vallejo, California, San Francisco, California, Los Angeles, California, and Inglewood, California, and we made sure we split the visiting time to visit both sides of the family.

Growing up in the city, with a hint of the country tending to the chicken, collecting the chicken eggs, picking vegetables from the garden, and feeding the dog in my grannies' backyard was peaceful. The experience of combining the city mixed with the essentials of a country atmosphere provided me the benefits of understanding joy, the joy that comes from God. The identification of life without any knowledge of wealth, riches, and prosperity granted me access to the simple life. Taking a long walk by Bachman Lake overlooking the still waters is always relaxing to me. As a small child the only stress I encountered was running from the snakes that crawled up into the garden from the Trinity River. Often, they made it all the way to the front yard, which faced the same skillful chopping by My Big Mama. Second dose of stress was induced from running from the roosters after I collected the eggs from the chicken coup.

Other than that, the beauty of the amazing blue sky with thick white clouds was the perfect escape, and it happened in my grannies' backyard. My first visit to the authentic country life being introduced to the water well, outhouse, farm animals, fishing, cleaning the fish, party lines[telephone system], the woods, the absence of street lights and a bathtub was all together different. The houses were so far apart from each other but the walk to visit was beneficial for health. The peaceful quietness reminded me of My Big Mama's back yard but the cows were right across the street, in front of Grandmother Ardie's home. I quickly learned how to speak the language of the cows, saying "Moo." Currently, I am a full-time student studying psychology. My plans are organized and documented to pursue new careers as a certified professional life coach, "God's Appointed Time Photography", and the creation of *"From Your Heart Greeting Cards."*

My first two main passions are Bible study and writing. Following is journaling, reading, performing arts, opera, symphony, theatrical performances, zoo, museums, attending the movies, travel, walking, dining, gardening, grocery shopping for certified organic fruits, and vegetables. I look forward to sailing, cruising across the seas, and traveling abroad. Only in my actual dreams have I visited India, Egypt, Africa, and Washington, D.C. Inside the dream I was standing inside the White House on September 1, 2002, and again on May 12, 2005, standing before My Big Mama in the wide hallway with red carpet. She spoke to me face-to-face for a long time.

All I remembered of that conversation was saying, "Yes Ma am," repeatedly. In the dream, I was scheduled to speak with the President of the United States while yet in the dream, I met with the President in a room with a large conference table. He was laughing and it was a joy speaking with him. The details of the communication are, likewise, sealed in the dream. Apparently, the nature of the communication was to remain unspoken. The revelation of the double dreams would be revealed later.

The dream was split into two parts because my cellular phone started ringing waking me up out of the dream. I turned the cellular telephone off as I was asking the LORD; please put me back into that dream. I closed my eyes and my request was granted.

I was back inside the dream, but I was in the United States House of Representatives. I stand to be corrected on the room but the seat I was assigned was in the near center on the third row. The entire row had a desk for writing. When the lady called the meeting to order, I had to change seats, and after the amazing incident that I have chosen to keep private. I was seated on the far left side of the room on the third row and in the third seat. As the meeting was being called to order by a female and everyone was standing. The moment she opened her mouth to speak things started to happen.

Again, I have chosen to seal that part of the dream. There on the floor across from my seat was a tall slender African American male over to the far left side. He was dressed in a white starched oxford shirt, and mauve khaki slacks with a brown wallet with brown leather dream half way out of his front left pocket. He was not able to speak because he was in a frozen stiff position but his eyes were open, whereas the meaning of that dream would be revealed later. I did not remember the details regarding the conception of the Declaration of Independence until I research the subject after the dream. Researching why My Big Mama appeared in the White House was something I desired to understand.

AND AFTER six days Jesus taketh Peter, James, and John his brother, and bringeth them up into an high mountain apart, And was transfigured before them: and his face did shine as the sun, and his raiment was white as the light. And, behold, there appeared unto them Moses and Elias talking with him. Then answered Peter, and said unto Jesus, Lord, it is good for us to be here: if thou wilt, let us make here three tabernacles; one for thee, and one for Moses, and one for Elias [Elijah]. While he yet spake, behold, a bright cloud overshadowed them: and behold a voice out of the cloud, which said, This is my beloved Son, in whom I am well pleased; hear ye him. And when the disciples hear it, they fell on their face, **and were sore afraid***. Matthew 17:1-6 [KJV]*

When the LORD speaks it alarms me to stand at full attention focusing on the words expressed. It happens when I least expect. I am not fearful all the time, but I will either jump up to make sure the bedroom door is locked, and even check inside my closet to see if someone made their way into my room while was I sleeping. Moses was buried by God, and Elias [Elijah] was carried away by a chariot and horses of fire and that happened in the Old Testament according to:

And it came to pass, as they still went on, and talked, that, behold, there appeared a chariot of fire, and horses of fire, and parted them both asunder; and Elijah went up by a whirlwind into heaven. And Elisha saw it, and he cried, My father, my father, the chariot of Israel, and the horsemen thereof. And he saw him no more: and he took hold of his own clothes, and rent them into two pieces. He took up also the mantle of Elijah that fell from him, and went back, and stood by the bank of Jordan; And he took the mantle of Elijah that fell from him and smote the waters, and said, Where is the LORD God of Elijah? And when he also had smitten the waters, they parted hither and thither: and Elisha went over. And when the sons of the prophets which were to view at Jericho saw him, they said, The spirit of Elijah doth rest on Elisha. And they came to meet him, and blowed themselves to the ground before him. 2 Kings 2:11-15 [KJV]

And Elisha prayed, and said, LORD, I pray thee, open his eyes, that he may see. And the LORD opened the eyes of the young man; and he saw: and, behold, the mountain was full of horses and chariots of fire round about Elisha. 2 Kings 6:17 [KJV]

When supernatural moments happen to those people which are chosen by God for the experience it comes from God. Samuel was chosen by God to hear his voice, while he was in the care of Eli:

*AND THE child Samuel ministered unto the LORD before Eli. And the word of the LORD was precious in those days; there was no open vision. And it came to pass at that time, when Eli was laid down in his place, and his eyes began to wax dim, that he could not see; And ere the lamp of God went out in the temple of the LORD, where the ark of God was, and Samuel was laid down to sleep; That the LORD called Samuel: and he answered, Here am I. And he ran unto Eli, and said, Here am I; for thou calledst me. And he said, I called not; like down again. And he went and lay down. And the LORD called yet again, Samuel. And Samuel arose and went to Eli, and said, Here am I; for thou didst call me. And he answered, I called no, my son; lie down again. Now Samuel did not yet know the LORD, neither was the word of the LORD **yet*** *revealed unto him. And the LORD called Samuel again the third time. And he arose and went to Eli, and said, Here am I; for thou didst call me. And Eli perceived that the LORD had called the child. Therefore Eli said unto Samuel, Go, lie down: and it shall be, if the call thee, that thou shalt say, Speak, LORD; for thy servant heareth. So Samuel went and lay down in his place. And the LORD came, and stood, and called as at other times, Samuel, Samuel. Then Samuel answered, Speak; for thy servant heareth. I Samuel 3:1-10 [KJV]*

Eli was a priest [I Samuel 1:9], and he made sure that Samuel was actually hearing from the voice of the LORD. Once Eli confirmed that the voice of the LORD was calling Samuel. he taught him the correct way to respond to the voice of the LORD.

Inside most of my dreams, I am often always barefoot, whereas, the sole of my feet touches the soil/ground. I have a taste for fine and finer things, which were conceived in dreams, and visions from the time Robert left for his deployment to Bosnia. My grannies' home was filled with fine antiques, shining hardwood flooring, and candelabra positioned, in the center of the formal dining room table. Everything was always in place because guests would visit all during the week and on the weekends. It was a place where many people felt right at home to dine and fellowship together.

My Uncle Marzuq [Muslim] is a prolific and effective speaker. My Big Mama was profuse with Bible knowledge breaking bread openly one-on-one as she prepared a fine meal at the table for each person. Passing by I would make a point to listen to her words. She was direct and with clarity but with an abundance of grace and consideration. I was also helping my grannies serve meals because the people came hungry and ready for stimulating conversation. I knew how to greet and serve the senior citizens' ladies who came one day out of each week for prayer. Nevertheless, the massive crowds that gathered on the weekend were hard work, but I enjoyed every moment. My Aunt Nellie Faye Taylor drove in from Vallejo, California, and when people heard she was coming to town the front and back yard was packed with people.

At the mentioning of California, I am reminded of the first time I stood on the seashore of Pismo Beach. I was thinking of My Big Mama wishing for her to witness the abundance of water, which the view was endless. I had never seen so much water. We had passed so much water along the way en route to California, and it was breathtaking. I knew about the Trinity River from the view of the backyard at my grannies. As we drove up to the beach, I jumped out of the vehicle running as fast as I could and when my feet touched the sand I stood there for a long time not moving on my own. I allowed the rushing in and out of the water to carry me closer into the water. The view was breathtaking. It was another metamorphosis experience from the limited view of the back yard to an endless view of water. I was enthralled at an amazing endless view. Even so, I knew she was back at home carrying on without my help. I thought of My Big Mama because I was missing being in her midst. I was hoping that she likewise was missing and thinking of me. Her unique style of sharing God's word was administered while the people were dining at the table. They could not help but to listen because the food was intensely savory. Every bite was delicious and dessert was waiting. If you asked me, My Big Mama and Little cooking skills were culinary, and I was the test kitchen tester. Little Mama never placed the homemade macaroni on the dining room until I would sing after the first bite. It was missing that potent flavor she knew I would tell her the truth, "Little Mama, it's missing something." She would say, "I know just what to add." The next test by me moved the large bowl to the formal dining room table.

I enjoyed watching My Big Mama and Little Mama team up at the dinner table breaking bread sharing the word of God with the people. Once you took at seat at the formal dining room table at my grannies home you knew the food was excellent, and the word and prayer would set the tone for the most enjoyable experience. My life growing up as a small child was a time of great mental wealth. All that I did not understand at the time, the fruition of revelation was seasoned by God at the appointed time.

Growing into my teens, I was introduced to my father's side of the family [brothers and sisters]. They grew up in Gary, Texas but relocated into various parts of California. They were prepared to live a life of enjoyment, which motivated me to think and live outside the box. Each year, summer vacation became extremely exciting. The moment we arrived in California, we were greeted by so many relatives waiting at my father's sister. Upon our arrival, the family stayed up all night talking. It was good that Uncle Kotee and Aunt Fayrene lived in a huge two story home, which accommodated so many relatives. I felt like a kid in a free candy store. I made sure I packed my little bag with my favorite wine candies before we left Texas.

Most of my uncle's in California were pastors and ministers of the gospel. I don't think they ever went to sleep when I woke up the house was filled with people, when I sent to sleep through the house being filled with people, which reminded me of My Big Mama's House. When I met my father's mother, I loved her so. Mother Ardie [Muh] was nurturing just like My Big Mama. She too talked about the LORD from sun up to sun down so I was always surrounded by godly women and men who loved God. My Aunt Annie Mildred from California is a talker and will stand up and shout about the goodness of God. Likewise, My Aunt Ora Lee, Uncle Joe B., and the list goes on. My cousin Gloria taught as a professor at UCLA, and she loves to sing and play the piano. My cousin Angela Blair is known for her singing abroad. My family history consists of the Byrd, Johnson/Pugh, Lilly, Choice, Jones, Clark, Turknett, Taylor, Dever, Franklin, Mitchell, Ingram, Banks, Wallace, Alcorn, and the last names go on. My family is scattered all over the United States.

I have a taste for finer things because I grew up with antiques, and I was exposed to mink coats, fine vehicles while observing my aunts, uncles, cousins, and relatives from California, Texas, and other states, which influenced my taste in tailored fashion and style. Uncle Glen's wife was always dressed from head to toe, which he was a minister of the gospel. They drove in from California to visit, in a luxury vehicle. I loved their sense of style. Uncle Glen's wife was soft spoken, graceful, and well-groomed.

From the time, I met Robert the military aviation combat pilot I started having dreams seeing mansions, estates, fine homes, few of the simple things I enjoy in life. I knew Robert owned an estate, but I never got a chance to visit his hometown because he was deployed to Bosnia, and I moved twice losing all of his information and forgetting his last name. Above all, attending worship service giving God thanks is top on my list, which includes prayer.

My favorite places I am looking forward to traveling, and visit is Tahiti [Bora, Bora], Hawaii, Venice, Italy, Jerusalem, Egypt, and Africa. One thing about me, I grew up and was raised in church, and I am planted. My pastor is Dr. Ervin D. Seamster Jr. Before I met him naturally. I met him in the spiritual realm, in 1985. I met him physically on May 27, 2007. Similar before Pastor Jakes became my pastor on September 1, 1996. Frequently, I heard his name flowing through the bank where I was employed.

The mentioning of his name during the day while working was synonymous with debits, credits, and balance. Not one day passed by without me hearing his name, the repeat of something he said, or where he was scheduled to appear for a conference. Therefore, I realized he was significantly different, and he was no ordinary preacher.

The segment went off and I missed his name, but I wondered what to make of the power that I felt. I had never felt that before from a pastor, preacher, or teacher. A few days later, I was upstairs pulling clothing from the dryer to fold, and I heard that voice, which sounded like that preacher. I kept the television on that same station hoping that he would preach again. Well, he did but I was upstairs.

I hurried to pull the clothing out of the dryer, and as I was running to step down the steep stairs inside my condo. I was half way down and I flipped and tumbled the rest of the way. My clothing from the dryer was all over the dining and kitchen floor, but I had to leave them there to catch what the preacher was saying. I felt that power again. It felt like invisible electricity. Standing there in amazement trying to understand what I was experiencing. It reminded me of the first time I heard the small still voice at age seven seated on those three steps of my grannies back porch. And it was similar to what I felt seated before my grannies each week during their weekly prayer meetings but the power had magnified. It was another dimension of power that I felt. I stood there in front of the television and missed his name again. I believe it was July 1996, when I experience a supernatural invitation through a visitation which followed with a telephone call inviting me to attend the Potter's House.

Through a compromise, I attended Sunday evening service at the Potter's House. I agreed to visit providing; she attended my morning worship service at my church. Afterwards, we enjoyed dinner at her home. She prepared a large pot of fresh mustard greens, yams, chicken and dressing with cake, and pie, which was all made from scratch. My compliments were offered to the chef, she is indeed a fine cook. We rested a few minutes after dinner and prepared to head to the Potter's House. Since, she picked me up to visit that was her insurance for me to attend her church without changing my mind. When I arrived at her church, we had to wait outside for a long time, and we were several hours early. I was terribly upset with her because I wore heels with four inches. Waiting in the car was out of the question, the reason was unknown to me.

However, I removed my shoes and I waited patiently, which later I understood her early arrival-the crowd increased massively with thousands of people. She was banking on a seat up close, which it was necessary to arrive early and wait. She dared not to inform me of the long wait, which she knew I would have missed visiting her new church. As we were waiting another gentleman drove into the parking lot. He was driving a brand new two-toned Lexus cream and tan exterior. I recognized him from a Church of God in Christ, which was located on the opposite end [east] of the street where I grew up as a small child. I would frequently visit by invitation with the Fall's family. He was a member.

As a small girl I watched him during Sunday service because he was different. He was distinctive, articulate, handsome, distinguished, and spiritual. Impeccable style and he was always well-groomed and with a quality mannerism. His custom tailored attire fit his athletic physique perfectly. Being tall and slender with the picture of strength was a compliment to his disposition. If I am not mistaken, he was a military soldier. His persona was personal and private. The gentleman was a worshipper. The following scripture speaks of a worshipper:

Now we know that God heareth not sinners: but if any man be a worshipper of God, and doeth his will, him he heareth. John 9:31 [KJV]

Study to shew thyself approved unto God, a workman that needeth not to be ashamed, rightly dividing the worth of truth. 2 Timothy 2:15 [KJV]

My people are destroyed for lack of knowledge: because thou hast rejected knowledge, I will also reject thee, that thou shalt be no priest to me: seeing thou hast forgotten the law of thy God, I will also forget thy children. Hosea 4:6 [KJV]

The four words that were spoken by God unequivocally stand. God's written word stands with me. I am rooted in the spirit and word of God. I made a decision this year to disarm the voices of people, which speak in opposition against God's word. Confidently, I am no longer willing to allow God's spoken or written words to be altered. If it was spoken and written by the Power of God, then I believe it. The situation with the woman in the garden of Eden became a case because she allowed the serpent to beguile her with modified communication of God's spoken commands. She listened to the voice of the serpent and compromised God's word.

And the LORD God commanded the man, saying, Of every tree of the garden thou mayest freely eat. But the tree of the knowledge of good and evil, thou shalt not eat of it: for in the day that thou eatest thereof thou shalt surely die. Genesis 2:16-17 [KJV]

It was difficult leaving my church, but it was time for me to go forward. Sometimes it may not feel nice but when it's time to move in a different direction, it's time to move. When it was time for Elijah to move the brook dried up and the word of the LORD came to Elijah:

And it came to pass after a while, that the brook dried up, because there had been no rain in the land. And the word of the LORD came unto him, saying, Arise, get thee to Zarephath, which belongeth to Zidon, and dwell there: behold, I have commanded a widow woman there to sustain thee. I Kings 17: 7-9 [KJV]

The steps of a good man are ordered by the LORD: and he delighteth in this way. Though he fall, he shall not be utterly cast down: for the LORD upholdeth him with his hand. Psalm 37:23 [KJV]

When we see people fall and make mistakes we have an accountability to pray for them without robbing them with vicious gossip. I was taught by My Big Mama and father to pull the weeds from the garden, which allowed the vegetable to grow effectively. I never mentioned those weeds again.

Therefore, judge nothing before the time, until the Lord come, who both will bring to light the hidden things of darkness, and will make manifest the counsels of the hearts: and then shall every man have praise of God. 1 Corinthians 4:5 [KJV]

Sharing positive communication and beneficial information is a delight. Conversing with people empowers me to transfer positive energy. If life tends to be a little clogged I retreat into a sabbatical to be refreshed. Hoping to avoid sharing any negative elements of my energy with people, I try to take it to the LORD who is able to take it from me completely. If I drop the weight of the matter on another person they may not be prepared to take it to the LORD. Therefore, I am thoughtful and mindful of the contents of my conversation with others and about others. Incidentally, I may not know or be aware when a person may have been forgiven by God, whereas God cast the sin/sins in depths of the sea. If I continue announcing the sin trying to bring it back to life, then I am committing an offense called sin. It is not my business to pull a sin out of the depths of the sea. It was placed there by God to be forgotten:

Who is a God like unto thee, that pardoneth iniquity and passeth by the transgression of the remnant of his heritage? He retaineth not his anger forever, because he delighteth in mercy. Micah 7:18 [KJV]

He will turn again, he will have compassion upon us; he will subdue our iniquities; and thou wilt cast all their sins into the depths of the sea. Micah 7:19 [KJV]

Pastor James Turknett called me over the telephone early one morning, and I had something on my mind, and I was angry about it.

His reply turned my focus to pray on my own. He used effective godly wisdom that critiqued me without insulting me. It took one divine appointed telephone call that reminded me to seek God. The subject never came up again. That call was about spiritual education concerning my future communication:

Wherefore, my beloved brethren, let every man be swift to hear, slow to speak, slow to wrath. James 1:19 [KJV]

People that give a quick answer to godly matters may often speak from their collection of stored wisdom not seeking a fresh understanding for a new day. They will speak over a fresh word from God with information from what they have stored in their mental storage over years.

They may give you a stale answer when God is giving you something new concerning his purpose and preparation, in your life. I meet very few people that will say, "I do not have an answer but I will pray and seek God." Most people will speak on the spot to answer God's purpose in a person's life. When people are puzzled or confused concerning God's Business, I have learned to encourage them to pray, fast if necessary, and wait upon the LORD. I am quick to say, "I have no comments."

When the LORD speaks a fresh word into my spirit, I will convey the message, but I refuse to deliver a stale dated message over a fresh word from God. I was previously a member of the Potter's House under the leadership of Pastor T. D. Jakes, from September 1, 1996 to April 14, 2007. I tried to go back on my own, but it was for me to remain at my new church home. God planted me, in a place for his purpose. What I learned from attending the Potter's House was for the continual spiritual journey. I needed to know more about God the Spirit, and I learned from the best. The knowledge and understanding that I received felt like a spiritual Ph.D., degree being awarded and sealed with spiritual substance for new journey. I walked into the Potter's House spiritually blind, but I walked out informed of spiritual information. The spiritual realm is real, which was seldom taught in my prior church background. If it was taught I was distracted and not focused missing the message. The knowledge is now applied extensively, which I am able to embrace the volume of the words recorded in scripture concerning principalities:

For we wrestle not against flesh and blood, but against principalities, against powers, against the rulers of the darkness of this world, against spiritual wickedness in high places. Ephesians 6:12 [KJV]

My Big Mama never mentioned the above scripture to me. When the attacks hit my life all I knew to do was pray. I understand that spirits transfer and I no longer wonder why a person act so bad or evil. A hard lesson learned is a lesson retained with godly wisdom.

Wherefore take unto you the whole armour of God, that ye may be able to withstand in the evil day, and having done all, to stand. Stand therefore, having your lions girt about with truth, and having on the breastplate of righteousness; And your **feet shod with the preparation of the gospel of peace**; Above all, **taking the shield of faith**, wherewith ye shall be able to **quench all the fiery darts** of the wicked. And take the helmet of salvation, and the sword of the Spirit, which is the word of God: Praying always with all prayer and supplication in the Spirit, and watching thereunto with all perseverance and supplication *for all saints*. Ephesians 6:13-16-18 [KJV]

On Father's Day, and special event, I visit the Potter's House. And sometimes I visit to say hello to my friends I acquired during those eleven years. The message is always potent. Equally, the LORD blessed me on June 3, 2007, to unite with a new church under the leadership of Dr. Ervin D. Seamster, Jr.

Any attempt to introduce you to him, may turn this book into being about him. God blessed his life with the gift of being an outstanding orator. His methodology to exegete the word of God is profound. If I were to write a book about my pastor, it would be titled "The Exegesis." The first time I heard him speak from the pulpit he was attired in a black robe, which I thought was a regular robe that preachers often dress. A few years later, the Monday group was showering him with appreciation and I thought about the first time I heard him preach wearing the black robe.

Thoroughly researching the meaning and elements associated with a doctorates' degree, it was apparent that I was under the leadership of a man of God with an extensive education that I could talk too and ask questions directly without holding my questions and hoping for an answer. His words exactly upon receipt of a Biblical question, "Johnson, open your bible to…"

Once the Bible was opened, I discovered the reason a young man name Manuel advised me to get under a leader I could talk to personally. He said, "You are rare, and you will need a close connection of communications with your pastor. There is more to you spiritually than what meets the eye." Listening to his word, I continued as usual but God interrupted my routine ordering my steps to be under the leadership of Dr. Seamster. I am certain I may take credit for any additional grey hair growing on his head.

One thing for sure, he is not afraid of my feisty disposition. I mean this in a nice way but most people back away from me because I need to go deeper in my understanding of the Bible. I tend to ask thought provoking questions. My pastor has answered most of my questions regarding the books of the bible from Genesis to Revelation thus far. My current knowledge of the Bible is challenged everyday from people that think and learn outside the box. When I encounter people graced with knowledge beyond my scope that is when I go into the research mode. Which, the next step is to speak to my pastor. If I do not understand the scripture or any element of the lesson during Bible study, I will raise my hand to ask him a question. I do not mind asking my pastor questions, but I prefer knowing information before going to him. Near the end of Bible study, he opens the floor with Q&A. When I have more than one question, asking the first question, may answer all my questions, whereas when he answers one question he will often provide a well-rounded answer covering other potential questions. If answering specific questions require him to get back with an answer, he is humble with humility to answer your questions during the next bible study.

I credit God for blessing my Pastor with intellectual knowledge and for allowing him to have a down to earth demeanor.

During worship service and Bible class, I am like a small kid in a free candy store. His collective, earned, and spiritual knowledge integrated with experience is empowering. Bible study is preparing me to improve my knowledge of the Bible and lifestyle immensely. I enjoy learning, understanding, knowing, and applying God's Word with godly wisdom. Before Pastor Noel Jones popularity propelled him into a national gospel icon, he was teaching per various church congregations here in Dallas, Texas. A young lady name Wanda Wigfall, which was my coworker where we worked side-by-side in Human Resources at the Pizza Inn Corporate Head quarters, which they were located on Stemmons Freeway and Inwood Road. Wanda was also one of my upper alumnae classmates from high school. She invited me to ride with her to hear a great speaker of the gospel. His name was Noel Jones. During that time, I believe he was residing in Longview, Texas. He was extremely tall, slender, and a preppy dresser. He spoke distinctively carefully selecting his words with excellent speech and articulation. I noticed his method of teaching was supported with handouts. As the audience followed his teaching, while observing the handout, he was a brilliant speaker. The church was small but the teaching from the Bible was a mountain top experience. He was teaching from the book of Revelation.

If memory serves me correctly, this was around the early 1980's or the end of the 1970's. I had just purchased a brand new mustard color Monte Carlo with the vinyl mauve top. He asked for my telephone number, so he could let me know when and where he was scheduled to speak, in Dallas, Texas. He mentioned that he lived with friends when they invited him to Dallas to speak. When he called to inform me of the church location I made sure I visited to hear him speak. He was profoundly philosophical then, and more so today. He called me one evening after I heard him speak, while he was still in Dallas, Texas. "Did you enjoy the teaching?" That was the first question he asked me. "Yes," I replied. Then he asked me to expound on the details [little did he know I was on my way out the door to a nice Jazz Club].

I recapped a few details of his teachings. Immediately, he said, "You need to go deeper in the word. There is more in you." I head his warning, but I was focused on getting ready for the Jazz Club. Overlooking his words of warning was the worst thing in the world I could have done. I missed my turning point, so I had to take the long road of learning to listen and obey God. Years later, when he stood before me on Thanksgiving Day at the Potter's House to deliver the Thanksgiving Day message, I did not recognize him nor did I remember him, but it was something about him that grabbed me.

Around or nearly fifteen years had passed, and I had no idea the messenger God used to warn me to go deeper was standing before me delivering the message addressed from the book of Job. I moved several times and I lost connections with Pastor Noel Jones. I forgot all about Noel, but I knew I would laugh about his first name thinking of the Christmas Carol. One day, while seated at my desk working at TXU Energy, I was taking a break, and I heard the small still voice instructing me to read the bio of Pastor Noel Jones that he was the same ministers who use to come up from Longview, Texas to teach in Dallas, Texas. I had a few minutes, and it was true.

When I met Robert on the freeway, I was a member of Oak Cliff Bible Fellowship. I started out with My Big Mama, Little Mama, and those twelve senior citizens ladies [weekly prayer meetings]. My first official pastor was Pastor Culpepper, which thereafter followed with Pastor, I. L. Finney, Brother Reginald B. Dulin, Dr. Tony Evans, Pastor T. D. Jakes, and my current pastor Dr. Ervin D. Seamster, whereas he carries the torch with an incredible methodology. When I met Dr. Seamster, he stood to preach on May 27, 2011, wearing a black robe, which was the first time I met and heard him preach. I had no idea he was living in my previous neighborhood on the opposite side and developing his ministry down the street from my condominium at the Bronco Bowl.

Reading about the robes of the priests and all the scripture concerning robes and especially the robe concerning Jesus was interesting. I desired to know more about the robe worn by my pastor. It was no ordinary robe. It was his doctoral robe. Likewise, I desired to understand the criteria of earning a Ph.D. Upon completing my research of the Doctor of Philosophy title. I discovered that I am under a leader blessed with a double portion of knowledge. He is an academically brilliant and filled with the Holy Ghost.

It was God's purpose to order my steps to be invited to attend his church. I listen to him intently Sunday after Sunday pulling up the roots of the Bible teaching us to examine the beginning of scripture to receive the meaning of scripture with distinction understanding the relevance for living life. He taught us to understand how rightly divide the word to know when and how the scripture is applicable to us. Another thing,

Surely, I believe it was determined for me to go on a spiritual journey, which I am not stuck in a tradition.

Gaining firsthand knowledge of a church or a person is personal but hearing about a church or a person is from a distance. I have learned to keep my mouth off people, errors, mistakes, and uneducated comments because if I am not talking directly to the person or praying about it-I may be in violation. People often repent in prayer so talking and casually gossiping is the wrong position for anyone to take. The same group gossiping may consider turning the communication into prayer and leaving it with God. Every time we feel the urge to talk about the situations of others, taking it to God is prayer is the right thing to do.

I cannot speak for everyone else, but I have learned how to locate the root of scripture. He allows us to take a self-examination at the evidence and to retain the knowledge of knowing. It was my pastor, which placed me in vital positions to be a participant in servitude. He trained me to operate expensive sound equipment and how to run, and manage a church bookstore.

When Dr. Seamster formed the Monday Night Class, with a hand-picked group of about seven people-I had no idea he was about to empower us with defined knowledge and tools for the being leaders. He taught us extensively biblical discipline. And he shared with us the book titled: LEADERSHIP ON THE LINE. He studied from the bible, and we studied real life experiences from this brilliantly written book. My pastor introduced us to the people, in the community, which we under the mission extended beyond the walls of the church building.

He helped us to understand the mission extended outside of the church walls. We knew that not all unchurched, hurting, broken, and isolate people will visit the church.

Meeting him was my full-circle and my church home. He is down to earth but a force to encounter. Meeting and talking with him encouraged me to return to college. Therefore, special thanks to my enrollment counselor See Vang, and academic counselor Whitney Radecacher for an abundance of encouragements and academic support to return to school. Higher Education is the medicine to obtain knowledge on a natural platform but the best education is noted in the scripture:

But the Comforter, which is the Holy Ghost, whom the Father will send in my name, he shall teach you all things, and bring all things to your remembrance, Whatsoever I have said unto you. John 14: 26 [KJV]

College math is fast approaching and I will soon experience my first flight on a jet. Therefore, I am standing on his scripture:

Peace I leave with you, my peace I give unto you: not as the world giveth, give I unto you. Let not your heart be troubled, neithter let it be afraid. John 14:27 [KJV]

I am planted by God, under the leader, whom I actually and literally I dreamed about in 1985. I dream dreams and I have learned to wait on the understanding, and the fruition. The last fifteen years of my life have been the most humbling experience. Furthermore, I learned the importance of waiting on the LORD with patience, which is why I never dated anyone after meeting Robert. I will be the first to tell you-I do not know what God is up to, but He is up to something. My steps are ordered by the LORD.

God is doing something new because I dreamed a dream of Robert on January 16, 2011, which led me to engage in a personal letter writing campaign to the military, a military attorney, , and a high government official without a response. Therefore, I am writing his book to Robert and about Robert because I believe this was the purpose of hearing

God's audible voice on Stemmons Freeway, and the dream on January 16, 2011, celebrating a forth coming victory.

I could write about all the negative things that happened in life, but there comes a time when the three scriptures below serve as a motto for living this life. I treasure these scriptures because they remind me of the turning point that is happening today:

Brethren, I count not myself to have apprehended: but this one thing I do, forgetting those things which are behind, and reaching forth unto those things which are before. Philippians 3:13-14 [KJV].

I press toward the mark for the prize of the high calling of God in Christ Jesus. Philippians 3:14 [KJV].

And we know that all things work together for good to them that love God, to them who are the called according to his purpose. Romans 8:28 [KJV]

Through dreams and visions, I learned where Robert was, so I sent an e-mail to the White House, the military attorney residing in Washington, D.C., and I wrote to the Pentagon addressing a particular general. The letter was returned with the name of the Lt. Gen., which the name was marked through. Waiting until a long time and hearing nothing from the White House, thinking my e-mail was among countless e-mail waiting to be read. It was time to write a book, which was confirmed upon receipt of an additional l returned letter unopened. I knew it was time to write the book and the rest is up to God.

Throughout the fifteen years after meeting Robert, I consistently read scripture, which a selection of scriptures are chronicled in this book. The more I read the scripture the easier it was waiting and not dating anyone for fifteen years. I went on a few dates, but I never dated anyone within those years. I never met anyone else like Robert. He was sent and sealed by God. As I read the scriptures, I developed a close connection to help me to wait upon the LORD. I felt it was important to provide a glimpse of my background to inform readers that I first heard the small still voice of God at age seven. As I matured, I understood God as Spirit.

Jesus walked on the earth talking with people for forty-days after the resurrection. When I speak of hearing of the voice of God, it means that God is alive.

Thus saith the LORD, thy Redeemer, the Holy One of Israel; I am the LORD thy God which teacheth thee to profit, which leadeth thee by the way that thou shouldest go. Isaiah 48:17 [KJV]

But the anointing which ye have received of him abideth in you, and ye need not that any man teach you: but as the same anointing teacheth you of all things, and is truth, and is no lie, and even as it hath taught you, ye shall abide in him. John 1:27 [KJV]

Which things also we speak, not in the words which man's wisdom teacheth, but which the Holy Ghost teacheth; comparing spiritual things with spiritual. 1 Corinthians 2:13 [KJV]

After that he appeared in another form unto two of them, as they walked, and went into the country. Mark 16:12 [KJV]

Because the carnal mind is enmity against God: for it is not subject to the law of God, neither indeed can be. So then they that are in the flesh cannot please God. But ye are not in the flesh, but in the Spirit, if so be that the Spirit of God dwell in you. Now if any man have not the Spirit of Christ, he is none of his. Romans 8:7-9 [KJV]

FOR THIS IS HE

eading the Bible about Samuel and David, helped me to master the understanding of how God will shine a spotlight on your life when you are focused on other things. When you least expect a blessing, a blessing is waiting for you. And when you are handpicked and chosen by God. It's a reason to be thankful and grateful knowing first hand that you are chosen by God. After the experience in September 1995, I pondered the words from the spiritual audible voice of God. On October 5, 2005, a tall and very handsome gentleman named Demetrius sat across from me in the aisle seat. Pastor Jakes was absent and the guest minister Dr. James Woodson taught. Wednesday Bible Study. He asked us to extend the aisle and hold hands for the corporate prayer. As we were extending into the aisles, the minister was talking in general about different thing giving us time to connect our hands.

Demetrius grabbed my left hand and stretched my short arm with the length of his long arm to the altar. I heard him praying before the corporate prayer started. Opening my eyes, when I heard him, saying, "LORD THIS IS SHE." I was the only person holding his hand, and there was no one on his left side. As I was straining standing on my tippy toe because he had my left arm stretched toward the altar, and I did not want to interrupt his prayer. A ladder would have been sufficient, so I could have stepped up a few steps to meet his height. As he was praying I had to open my eyes to look at him, and he had his eye closed, and it appeared that he was praying diligently. Respectfully, he was the most handsome gentleman, at the Potter's House. Well, Demetrius and my friend Joe from New York are both very handsome gentlemen. Demetrius stood about 6 feet 4 and Joe, stands at 6 feet 3. I know because once Joe had me to go and get Demetrius, so he could meet him. And as they stood before each other, Demetrius was taller than Joe. Joe advised that Demetrius was 6 feet 4, and that he was 6 feet 3. I was standing next to Demetrius about to faint because Joe said something to Demetrius concerning me.

Joe started laughing and they had no idea that I hyperventilate. Joe was still laughing and Demetrius had gone back to his seat way up in the front. Joe sat next to me teasing me about how I was trembling. I never told him that I hyperventilate. I did not expect to get that excited by a surprise and my brown bag was at home. I met Demetrius after graduating from God's Leading Lady Enrichment Program. As I was walking into the glass doors the next Sunday morning, he stood in line, as if he was a greeter. He grabbed my hand looking down into my eyes with a smile. He would not let my hand go. So I smiled and politely jerked my hand loose. Not long after that incident, he was seated across from me during Wednesday Night Bible Study on October 5. When he finished his prayer Dr. Woodson immediately started praying, the young lady on my right heard him, and she squeezed my hand so tight until it was hurting. I was wearing a ring on my left hand. I had to break from the prayer to inform her that she was hurting my hand. Perhaps she was trying to let me know that he was up to something. We took our seats and Dr. Woodson said, "Be sure to hug the people on both sides. I looked at Demetrius perplexed about his prayer and I did not get up to go and hug him. But I greeted the lady on my right with a smile.

Dr. Woodson was into his lesson, and suddenly he looked into my face and said, "It was your grandmother that anointed you." I jumped straight from my seat to acknowledge his spoken words. I was thinking at that precise moment, that My Big Mama had anointed me as a small child. Demetrius was watching. The following Sunday morning I was seated with Sister Ola, and we were discussing the rise of electricity with Sister Kathy, [the school teacher]. I was seated to the right of Ola relaxed because had about an hour before worship service started. I had my left arm around the back of her pew listening to them talk. The church pretty much empty and the pews in front of us were empty. I felt someone touch me, saying "Excuse me ladies.

I was wearing a mahogany mink hat, matching mink cuffs, and a Jones New York two piece suit, which was a gift. It was told outside and we were trying to thaw out. Since he made his way all the way down the pew-I decided to speak, saying, "Hello, how are you?" The incident with him praying, saying, "Lord, this is she," helped me continue in prayer not to trust everyone spoken and deeds of men. Things are not always what they appear to be from the surface. I have learned to ask God about secret agenda's and hidden motives. Read about how the woman in the garden of Eden was beguiled is enough for me to seek God about everything. The enemy is always up to something thinking he is clever and unnoticed. God be watching and knowing his every move. I never had the chance to ask Demetrius if he was sincere or to whom was he speaking the prayer. As a lady of class and mental distinction-I thought it was best to ponder. People knew not anyone could capture my attention, so they may have sent the very best. However, if it's not from God it is considered a counterfeit.

It was puzzling. He said, "Very well thank you." I wanted to know his name just for the record, and I knew how to ask. "My name is Linda, and your name is?" "My name is Demetrius." "It's a pleasure to meet you Demetrius." "No the pleasure is all mine." As he spoke to Ola and Kathy, he stepped into the aisle and said, "Two beautiful ladies," Ola and I enjoyed the compliment, and we continued to talk, but I was laughing on the inside. What he did was cute letting me know he was interested or having some fun. I joined my new church on June 3, 2007. I missed watching Demetrius praise the LORD with his long arms extended high as he could reach. The reason he came down my pew was for me to take notice to him. I would have been the first to tell him that he was a charming gentleman, but I must admit. I like when a man is shy, mean, and acts like a kid even when he is one of the great authority. Even so, after awhile it gets old. I do not know if he was serious or not so I stayed in my place as a woman of God and said nothing to him about his words. I continued to speak to him and greet him accordingly.

When I visit the Potter's, I always made sure I spoke to him. He is a really nice person and my god son [grandson] Marlund adores him. One Sunday after worship service he had a gift for Marlund, which was a large lifesaver. Marlund loved it. He came out of nowhere and gave it to Marlund. I have noticed him throwing his authority around from time to time. A few days after October 9, 2005, I found the scripture where the LORD told Samuel, "For this is he. [I Samuel 16:12-13]" It seems that God speak four powerful words to point someone out. He spoke four words to point out Robert, saying. HE IS YOUR HUSBAND. I will always cherish those spoken words.

I dreamed several dreams about Demetrius but one of the dreams I found to be interesting was the dream where I was seated on a picnic blanket with Demetrius watching the parade. We were seated outside on beautiful green grass, in an exclusive neighborhood watching a parade. He spotted Supreme Justice Clarence Thomas. He walked down to the parade, and he spoke to him. It was as if they knew each other. He came back saying, "He can really sing." I woke up wondering why I was seeing Supreme Court Justice Clarence Thomas. I was informed this year that Demetrius recently married a beautiful young lady.

And Samuel said unto Jesse, Are here all thy children? And he said, There remaineth yet the youngest, and, behold, he keepeth the sheep. And Samuel said unto Jesse, Send and fetch him: for we will not sit down till he come hither. And he sent, and brought him in. Now he was ruddy, and withal of a beautiful countenance, and goodly to look to. And the LORD said, Arise, anoint him: **for this is he**. *Then Samuel took the horn of oil, and anointed him in the midst of his brethren: and the Spirit f the LORD came upon David from that day forward. So Samuel rose up, and went to Ramah. I Samuel 16:12-13 [KJV]*

David was handpicked by God to replace Saul as king. I was inspired to share a unique experience that happened in September 1995, when I dreamed on January 16, 2011. Over a period of fifteen years, I rested dated anyone has mainly because of the audible words spoken by God concerning a husband. When Samuel received instructions from the LORD to go to Jesse the Bethlehemite: for the LORD had shone the spotlight on David to be the next king [1 Samuel 16:1 KJV].

The LORD never called out David's name nor any particular details concerning his identity, features, age, occupation, assignment, duties, nor his resume, which he killed a lion and a bear. Samuel the prophet embarked upon an interesting journey en to Jesse's house without any form identity of the person he was instructed to anoint with the horn of oil one of the sons of Jesse. The LORD said, I will shew thee what thou shalt do: and thou shalt anoint unto me him whom I name unto thee [I Samuel 16:3 KJV].

Speaking for myself. I can count the number of times I looked at the first man and accepted him to be a potentially suitable husband for life. Samuel had to interview Eliab [*firstborn*], Abinadab [*second*], Shimma [*third*], Nethaneel [*fourth*], Raddai [*fifth*], Ozem [*sixth*], and David, which he was the *seventh* son according to. I Chronicles 2:13-15, and I Samuel 16:6-10 KJV. David was in the back keeping the sheep. David was about to be overlooked until Samuel took a stand, speaking to Jesse, saying, The LORD hath not chosen these [I Samuel 16:10 KJV].

Samuel's assignment was neither a difficult nor a complex assignment, but he had to depend on the continual guidance of the LORD for directions:

Trust in the LORD with all thine heart; and lean not unto thine own understanding. In all thy ways acknowledge him, and he shall direct thy paths. Be not wise in thine own eyes: far the LORD, and depart from evil. Proverbs 3:5-8 [KJV]

It's so easy to leave God out of the equation of living life and making decisions. I am guilty of starting my days without praying, granted that, I felt naturally that I was making wise decisions, but I walked into a number of pits. The pits which were custom and tailor made for me, which taught me to pray. I pray when I rise, during the day, and before I retired for bed at night. Honestly, Living life without prayer cost me to many years, precious times, and an abundance of heartaches.

Growing up in the midst of prayer warriors helped me to return to the foundation of prayer. Living life without communicating with God was out of the question. Therefore, prayer is included in my lifestyle.

Pray without ceasing. 1 Thessalonians 5:17 [KJV]

I cannot afford to allow a day to pass by without praying and praying for others. If I live my life in such a way, I will become selfish, self-centered, and careless to empower other people through prayer. When I pray, I am mindful that God is able to meet the need. He is omnipresent, omnipotent, omniscient, and pansophical. People all over the world need prayer. I spoke to Brother Noah, which is one of the ministers from my church that I desired to join the prayer ministry.

Prayer is released early every morning first my men of the church, and then the women. I have served in the sound room, book store, and my pastor allowed me to learn how to operate expensive sound equipment, and operate a church bookstore. I will willingly serve in any capacity but my passion is praying. Early Morning Prayer with the saints of God reminds me of the weekly prayer meetings with my grannies and those twelve ladies, which were seasoned senior citizens. If anyone asked me to describe them, that are simple, they were committed and dedicated prayer warriors.

I had a praying grandmother, well grandmothers and a community of collective prayer warriors who prayed for people. The time is of essence to stop gossiping and start praying. People are hurting all over the world, and payer is in demand. Innumerable ladies are hoping to marry the man who God had ordained to be their husbands. I have never been married, but I hope to be a powerful wife honoring my husband, my appointed husband and always willing to cover him in prayer. My desire is to kneel, bow, lay prostrate on the floor and pray with my husband leading prayer. I have no plans to stop praying for my husband. Marriage is a profound institution where two people are joined together in holy matrimony. The spirit of agreement in a marriage ordained and appointed by God, is a blessed marriage.

When Samuel looked upon Eliab, and said, Surely the LORD's anointed is before him.

But the LORD said unto Samuel, *Look not on his countenance, or on the height of his stature; because I have refused him: for the LORD seeth not as man seeth; for man looketh on the outward appearance, but the LORD looketh on the heart. 1 Samuel 16:6-7 [KJV]*

David was anointed by Samuel but his father Jesse made seven of his sons to pass before Samuel. However, Jesse spoke up asking if there were any other children knowing that none before him was chosen by God [I Samuel 16:10-11]. Throughout this book, you will read where I met several suitable gentlemen and only to name a few, they were not anointed and appointed by God for me. Looks, material things, status, gift, kind words, compliments, and deceitful communication are deceiving when contemplating a potential mate. I knew to wait and pray for my steps are ordered:

The steps of a good man are ordered by the LORD: and he delighteth in his way. [Psalm 37:23 KJV]

Samuel nearly made a mistake looking on the outer appearance of Eliab, saying, Surely the LORD's anointed is before him. The LORD interrupted him, saying, Look not on his countenance, or on the height of his stature; because I have refused him; for the LORD seeth not as man seeth; for man looketh on the outward appearance, but the LORD looketh on the heart [I Samuel 16: 6-7].

Writing this book was the last thing I desired to write about but a young lady shared a response from a personal prayer I posted on Streaming Faith, which is a popular Internet site. I posted a prayer concerning Robert. I posted the prayer after I thought I saw Robert standing over me at the Potter's House on March 14, 2010. I shared the experience of meeting Robert on Stemmons Freeway, September 1995 and what happened the morning of September 1995. Likewise, I shared the experience that happened during Sunday morning worship service with the tall gentleman whom I thought was Robert. She responded to me saying, "This must be written in a book." I smiled and said to myself, "No way."

I buried the idea of writing about Robert because I forgot and lost his last name, along with all the information he gave me. This is one reason I dislike living in an apartment or condo where management had the right to gain access when the tenant is at work. I thought about changing the locks where they would have to call me before entering.

Everyone cannot be trusted. Money had/have a way of gaining access without your knowledge. I assumed by my own assumption that Robert was killed in Bosnia. But for one quick moment during Sunday Morning Service at the Potter's House on March 14, 2011, changed everything. Apparently, it was a prelude of the forth coming dream I was about to experience on January 16, 2011.

I thought it was Robert standing in the north center aisle looking at me. There was one seat available next to me on my right. The gentle was dressed in a designer navy blue pin stripe suit, and he looked exactly like Robert. We gazed into each other's eyes for at least two straight minutes. I froze and was not able to move or speak to offer him the seat.

The usher stood still not understanding the eye contact between two people she looked straight ahead. Seconds away from the start of worship service, the debonair gentleman quickly dashed in directly behind me finding an empty seat on the next pew. He was seated to my immediate right about three people down.

I was trying to decipher the renewed refreshed feeling because it happened suddenly as he was standing there in the aisle before I turned to determine who was near with the similar aura of Robert, and if the gentleman looking into my eyes was Robert. It felt exactly as it did on Stemmons Freeway in September 1995. Looking through my peripheral he was looking at me. I was dressed casual and he was impeccably dressed. The moment was awarded because I was not at my best because I barely made it to worship service. I grabbed a lime jacket and a blue jean skirt and slide my feet into my mules with a three inch heel. My hair was combed but I was not in the right frame of mind to speak to him.

When I drove into the parking lot I thought to continue driving around to exit. Walking inside the glass doors I decided to turn around to go back home, but I turned back around and walked into the sanctuary and took a seat reading my Bible to take my thoughts off my deceased brother. Recently losing my eldest brother Michael, and I was not able to feel life because I never had a chance to grieve his crossing over. I am learning discipline when it comes to a person taking that final breath of life. Nevertheless, it was someone very close to me, and it happened suddenly on February 11, 2010, on the day Dallas, Texas was covered in thick blankets of pure white snow. The night before I learned of his death my heart was beating so fast as if it were about to explode, which was not normal for me.

I am careful of my salt intake, which I only use a hint Himalayan Pink Crystal sea salt with lemon juice. I kept praying and it did not stop until around 3:30am when I woke up out of a dream. It suddenly stopped. The telephone rang at 6:30am and I knew something was wrong seeing my mother's telephone number that early in the morning. She found my brother on the floor, and the paramedics were working on him. It was his heart. He mentioned to my mother that the doctors told him that his heart was about to explode.

He was scheduled to be admitted to the hospital on the next day, but he passed away early that morning. I saw someone in a dream crossing over near the back corner of the fence but there was a blanket of a white show. When I woke it the time was 3:30am. Running to the back door to look out; there was thick white snow everywhere, and it was beautiful. So I jumped back into bed and went back to sleep. The strength I used came from God because on the inside, I was not able to feel life. It was God giving me strength.

Seated in Sunday Morning Worship Service at the Potter's House on March 14, 2010, I sat quietly reading my bible before the start of service. The sanctuary was filled to capacity, and if you found the seat on the floor you were fortunate.

As I was reading my bible, I suddenly felt a powerful aura touch the bottom of my feet, which spread up to my head, and I was quickly refreshed. One moment I was fighting back tears to being rejuvenated. It felt like the same prodigious aura I felt coming from Robert when I met him on Stemmons Freeway. I turned my head slowly to the left and much to my surprise. there was this very tall distinguished gentlemen standing in the aisle looking straight into my eyes. My air supply cut off, and I stopped breathing, which means I was hyperventilating. No words, no movement, no air, and no one new to push me or give me a brown paper bag.

It happened once right in front of my new pastor Dr. Seamster, and he grabbed me causing my air to flow again. He was introducing me to his college classmates from one of his alma maters putting me on the spot. So many came to visit that Sunday Morning Worship service to hear him speak, which was a special service. When he called me out in the front of them, I stopped breathing. I was not able to take a step forward, nor inform him that I needed a brown paper bag to breathe. My mouth was hanging wide open frozen, and I could not feel my knees, which meant I was about to hit the floor hard, in the front of all those people standing around in the east foyer.

He suddenly grabbed me pulling me directly in front of the couple he was trying to introduce me to. I wanted to tell him, "Thank you," but he was making his point to them about me, and all my e-mails I would send to him with Biblical information. I never shared with him my problem with hyper ventilation. He knew what to do, likewise, a young lady standing behind me as I was crowned high school queen-I stopped breathing from the sudden announcement that I was the new high school queen over the entire school. I was to take my walk after being crowned, robed and honored with a dozen long-stem red roses. She gently pressed her hand in the center of my back, and I took a step.

Shaking like a leaf with each step and I was praying that I did not faint in the front of all those people cheering me on. My felt so lightheaded and I knew it was a matter of seconds before my body embraced the floor. We grew up together as small children with so many memories. He was my protector because my father passed away, in 1975, and my Uncle Robert "Alcon" Choice Jr. passed away on June 19, 1978. I considered him as my father, and I called him if anything went wrong. Likewise, Robert, the military aviation combat pilot, My Uncle Robert served in the military. His father was named Robert Alcorn, from Betty, Texas. My Aunt Clarkie, his widow, and my mother informed me today of family I never met. We live in a small world with a plethora of family secrets.

He lived thirty years of his life without knowing his real father until his natural father was on his death bed. Uncle Jr. [Robert] looked out for me after my father passed away. My brother Jr. was the eldest before his death. When he passed away and my brother Michael moved into the position as the eldest brother. I had to learn to acknowledge the Holy Ghost as my protector.

It was good that I had to wait for Robert because it taught me patient and how to hold to God's spoken word. Interesting, after the dream on January 16, 2011, I begin to share the situation about Robert. The same questions were asked, repeatedly, "What if you never see him again?" I laughed within because I understand Isaiah 55:11. Furthermore, I focused on the three Hebrew boys: Shadrach, Meshach, and Abednego in the fiery furnace. Waiting on the LORD for my husband helped me to walk in the right direction. Robert shared something deeply intimate with me concerning his life, which while he was speaking tears ran down his cheeks.

Over the span of fifteen years not dating is an appointed validation of trust. The restoration and magnitude of trust a man hopes to acquire when he is married. I am so thankful to God for keeping me. Most of my time is spent in church, school, Bible study, writing, walking, watching movies, and visiting my family, friends, and engaging in other productive activities. With Robert serving in the military, he is subject to be deployed and away from home for long periods of time. When he comes home to surprise me, I rather he found me in engaging in a godly activity. Keeping busy is no problem. If I lived in the same state as his mother, I would spend time with her, while he was serving in active duty. I rather not marry, then end up marrying the wrong person living a miserable unhappy life. Meeting Robert on Stemmons Freeway was unexpected. When I think of how I met Robert, I think of *reaping what you sow*.

Be not deceived; God is not mocked: for whatsoever a man soweth, that shall he also reap. Galatians 6:7 [KJV]

For verily I say unto you, That many prophets and righteous men have desired to see those things which ye see, and have not seen them; and to hear those things which ye hear, and have not heard them. Hear ye therefore the parable of the sower. When any one heareth the word of the kingdom, and understandeth it not, then cometh the wicked one, and catcheth away that which was sown in his heart. This is he which received seed by the way side. But he that received the seed into stony places, the same is he that heareth the word, and anon with joy receiveth it; Yet hath

he not root in himself, but dureth for a while: for when tribulation or persecution ariseth because of the word, by and by he is offended. He also that received seed among the thorns is he that heareth the word; and the care of this world, and the deceitfulness of riches, choke the word, and he becometh unfruitful. But he that received seed into the good ground is he that understandeth it; which also beareth fruit, and bringeth forth, some an hundredfold, some sixty, and some thirty. Matthew 13:17–23 [KJV]

MANAGING A MARRIAGE

*T*ime passed and I grew up. Summer after summer I missed My Big Mama. I yet miss her today. She was my granny, and she was my best authentic friend. Watching how the couple related to each other was a secret observation. Some of the married couples were always arguing, which I knew was not for me. My assignment was to observe how each couple managed their marriages and families. There was not much affection, except for one couple that lived on the other block. A few of the wives always looked so nice and neat when they stepped out the door. And there were those that I felt were too comfortable with their personal appearance. Each home had a story and chapters being written. Admitting the Fields family was my favorite because there seemed to be order, structure, and excitement, in their family. I loved all the families, in my neighborhood. Walking down the street greeting each family was a refreshing experience. Best of all, the preparation of the families' evening meal filled the air with the aroma of food. Everyone in our neighborhood started preparing supper around the same time. The aroma of delicious foods saturated the streets, and they all were excellent cooks.

Unequivocally, My Big Mama was the best cook in the neighborhood. I am not just saying because she was My Big Mama. Simply, no one would match your caliber of seasoning, and cooking. If her food was awful trust me, I would tell the truth. While working at the bank I receive an early morning incoming telephone while working at the bank. The gentleman on the other end of the telephone was a bank officer from a different bank. Originally, his call was concerning business but upon hearing the sound of my voice, he said, "I like to meet you." "Meet me to date me or to have lunch?" "I would like to know you better to date you. " He said. My morning started with a bang. The sound of his voice was articulated and intellectual. He describes himself to me, since he was very tall and athletically fit.

Determining he had no problems finding a date, but I felt compelled to ask him if he were married. It was difficult thinking that he was single. The sound of his voice was soothing and charming. "May I ask you a question?" "Sure," he answered. "Are you married? His reply was, "Yes." Recently, attending a marriage seminar with Dr. Ocho, who was one of the assistant pastors from the mega church I previously attended. He was conducting the seminar. Being single, I had to ask for permission to attend. It was important for me to know more about marriage from a group setting. Involved in the Single's Ministry I disliked being in the atmosphere feeling I was on display. When people notified me that several young gentlemen were interested in meeting me-I made sure I left bible study early and missed the next Friday.

The bible study was effective, but I did want to reject anyone saying, "I am not interested and I refused to share my experience on Stemmons Freeway. The gentlemen were spiritually suitable to date but my heart was with Robert. Not willing to explain the supernatural to anyone. I stopped attending the single ministry all together. As far as I was concerned, I was Robert's spiritual wife appointed by God. Secretly planning for the appointed wedding ceremony-I clipped out pictures from wedding magazines and kept a picture journal of wedding ideas.

My understanding of a wife was that she was chosen by the man. Knowing that I was chosen and appointed it was essential for me to know how to be a virtuous woman and a virtuous wife. Hearing the audible voice changed everything. I heard the audible voice of God speaking, saying. HE IS YOUR HUSBAND. I did not talk about my encounter with people. I shared it with Karen, Janet, and Thomas but Karen, and Janet was the only two I told about the audible voice. Janet was planning her wedding to Cleo. I shared with Mother Jenkins that I had met Robert on Stemmons Freeway, but I pondered the supernatural words communicated.

Karen was my next door neighbor, and she would share a few things. Nevertheless, other than that I kept the supernatural words spoken by God's voice to myself. My quest was to know how to be a good spiritual wife. Therefore, I disliked a single man looking at me from across the room during bible study. I refused to visit the designated home of approve outing for the group. Most of the single gentlemen lived in fine homes, financially stable, and sold out to Christ. My heart and my thoughts were on the words spoken by the audible voice of God concerning Robert. Pondering God's words I made my request to attend the marriage seminar. It was not easy for me to talk about the audible voice of God speaking in my car, so I pondered and pursued to learn to be a wife.

Possibly, Dr. Ocho probably wondered why I desired to attend, and I was not willing to share the supernatural experience with him. Hypothetically thinking, Dr. Ocho may have enlightened me with spiritual insight, but instead I pondered the details. Thankful he did not ask because I might have missed the seminar and then maybe not, but I was not willing to take that chance. Forever thankful, he granted me access, and I was there, in attendance. I listened to every word he spoke, and every illustration he formulated to bring a visual understanding helping the married couples to elevate in marriage. Thinking he was handing them spiritual verbal glue, and they were sticking together so I tuned in intently. Since I was single and all the couples attending were married. Respectively, I learned from a theatrical presentation unscripted. Dr. Ocho featured the meaning of empathy. During those hours, he opened up the meaning of empathy, and the couples received the clarity, whereas they became the meaning. Watching them transform with a refreshed glow looking into each other's eyes with appreciation and love.

I desired to experience the reconciliation of a renewed metamorphosis of true love shared between two people united. At the end of the seminar, prayer was offered over the married couple and of course me the only single female in the group. Once the prayer was spoken, I decided to leave to allow the married couples to embrace each other in the moment of celebrating.

Although I desired to remain to witness the sealing of an amazing ending it was proper and respectful of the couples to enjoy their reaffirmed martial relationships, in the likeness of marriage. I made my exit quietly honoring the renewed healing. Unequivocally, marriage counseling is an asset to couples anticipating marriage or currently married. After the wedding ceremony, tomorrow and the next day will come. With each new day couple learn to management uniting as husband and wife. I realized a marriage goes beyond the excitement of being in love and living under the same roof. Married couples must learn to manage interference, distractions, changes, and attacks.

Consequently, the first three months of marriage are what I consider the merger of two people with idiosyncrasies becoming as one. Two people sharing their lives in the same space with respect, acceptance, and the benefit of appreciating compromises to agree to be a method I plan to incorporate into my marriage. Dr. Ocho taught me the meaning of effective communication always seeking a peaceful solution. The pre-marital counseling is a start as in elementary school. Elementary school does not prepare the student to live as an adult.

Elementary school was designed for the early stages of childhood. Middle school was strategically organized for the next level of learning catering to the early teenage years, which I believe is the massive discovery period required a commitment of supervision from parents. The body speaks so many languages and a child I believe required the knowledge of what is happening inside the body. Knowing and understanding the change, equips the child to manage the body and not be tricked into living a sinful life. Restraints with knowledge help to preserve the rights of being a child of God with a pure heart, and maintaining clean hands. Winning the war between the flesh and the spirit:

This I say then, Walk in the Spirit, and ye shall not fulfill the lust of the flesh. For the flesh lusteth against the Spirit, and the Spirit against the flesh: and these are contrary the one to the other: so that ye cannot do the things that ye would. But if ye be led of the Spirit, ye are not under the law. Galatians 5:15-18 [KJV]

When I was in my early teens I thought for a minute that I was able to make my own decisions. I was wrong, I did not know enough about life to properly manage my future. The wisdom of sensible and practical parents more lives on experiences. They may not share every detail with us but our parents can spot trouble a mile away. "He or she is the bad company," is what you may have heard followed with instructions to abort the relationship immediately. I had no choice but to discontinue the association or risk not being able to perform my cheerleading obligations. We thought we were half grown and able to govern our lives without our parents, but I believe this is the time when parents are able to influence the child to learn discipline with effective parenting skills.

With each new level of growth and changes knowledge of the changes and additions are vital elements to understand. Especially in a marriage, which I believe the first three years of marriage is the perfect time to schedule a third marital counseling session. Taking a preventive approach beforehand of a any unforeseen marital problems versus waiting for the storms to surface. I hope to engage in preventive martial counseling combined with a praying lifestyle. I want to know what he might deem as pleasing verses detestable about a woman. I understand everything will not be revealed during the first years of the merger of marriage. Understanding the essential elements are important to me as a single wife [I am a wife to emanate into the effective role of a wife]. I absolutely must take a journey into his spiritual and natural DNA. I need to study the science of him, and God will provide the spiritual proclivities of his creation-the nature and ego of the man is important to me. If I understand his nature and his ego, I may be able to cross the bridge with him. I hope to understand and avoid misunderstandings in the long-term of a marriage. Most people wait until they are in trouble but including an early preventive measure is a worthy invitation.

When couples pray individually, and pray together they put God first continually. Concerns will surface even between a praying couple but listening to people that are negative, bitter and those with a bad experience with marriage might not offer the right advice. Godly, wisdom and Holy Ghost discernment is the characteristics I may search for in a marital counselor.

Hoping the counselor realized that they do not have all the answers but the answers are with God. I believe a spiritual counselor is trained with in-depth knowledge of psychology, sociology, and biblical knowledge incorporated succinctly. So that, they are able to recognize and educate couples with essential information to hire and employ to achieve life changing result. Keeping God as the center focus is the disciplined balance for the journey. I fully support the acquired skills, knowledge, and hopefully experienced in spiritually Holy Ghost filled counselors to guide a married couple into biblical knowledge.

For example, if I should take a seat facing a counselor with my mate or potential mate-I hope to hear the counsel suggest we go before God in prayer before we break into the knowledge of man. Otherwise, I might suggest to my mate that we excuse ourselves and seek a praying counselor, whom is able and ready to acknowledge God first. Everything in life requires management, proper management. If we neglect to manage any aspects of living life, the results will be reflected in a deficiency. When I marry, I plan to schedule marriage counseling before we marry, after the first three months, the first year, at the end of three years, ten years, twenty years, and fifty years of marriage. Figuring after fifty years together is enough time invested to continue.

The logic behind the counseling is preventive and shares the excitement of marriage. Counseling should be a time to celebrate and not always to heal a broken marriage and one that are falling apart. Life requires management, and living life requires strategic management. Many of our parents receive only an elementary education, and they did alright. However, others may have suffered handicaps in the absence of higher learning or greater knowledge. Many parents are an absence for whatever reason, therefore, leaving the child or children to figure matter without adult supervision. However, a praying family facing any form of inadequacies knew to pray knowing that God will make a way. Surely, you have heard of one person in a family finally attending and graduating from college.

Prayer is essential because it is how we communicate with God our creator. Parents were vessels God used to bring us into this world, and we communicate with our parents. One should ask the questions of who created my parents, which is clarification that God is our creator. People make it over with prayers. Prayer warriors are praying daily interceding on behalf of others that do not have a clue some are praying for them in spite of their lifestyle and beliefs.

The importance of a disciplined lifestyle that included prayer as a lifestyle, including empathy is a benefit to incorporate into our daily lives. Not knowing that I would use what I learned in the seminar on the first business day of the week at work. It was early Monday morning, I took a seat at my desk, and the telephone started ringing. It was a call from a trust officer from another bank. As I was recording his request to assist with his inquiry, he said, "I like to know you better." His words were soothing, but I felt compelled to ask him if he were married. "Do you mind if I ask you a question?" "Sure," he replied. "Are you married?" He answered, "Yes." "Are things not happy at home?" He opened up a flood of frustrating concerns about his wife and all I could was listen until it was out of his storage. It was best that I heard it versus one that was ready to violate his married. He disliked the way she looked around the house wearing old robes, old gowns, and looking tired all the time with her hair un-kept, and wearing clothing with holes. Apparently, she was feeling relaxed around her husband but failed to recognize a woman is different compared to a man. Men are visual and there is nothing we can do to change the fact. I believe a married couple must grow together in that type of comfort for a man to see you at your very worse. Personally, I rather know more about my silent unspoken words. I rather he opened up and tells me at first glance that he is not happy seeing me walk around the house wearing an old war out robe. I like brand new pretty Victorian robes, gowns and expensive lingerie. I shared with him everything I liked. I instructed him to go out and purchase for his wife before she came home from work today. As he was taking notes, I instructed him to purchase her three different robes.

One for the bathroom with pretty matching terry cloth slippers. Another robe with a matching gown for the bedroom with the pretty matching slipper with a two-inch heel, and an additional Victorian robe and gown that were beautiful with again, the matching slippers where it could be possible serve as a lounger. He was quiet, "Are you taking notes?" I asked. "Yes, I am taking notes. " Purchase her several lingerie items the kind that you would like to see her wear, expensive perfumes that are pleasing to your senses, assorted French soaps, bath gels, creams, and whatever you see that you would like to see on and around your wife purchase it for her.

To seal the new beginning purchase some fresh cut flowers and present them to her. We hung up talking over the telephone, and I started trying to do my work. Nevertheless, I prayed for him that God would guide him to select the perfect items for his wife. I pray to God. I maintain nice essential to dress and adorn myself around my husband. I must rather see him at his worst then he sees me at my worse because I believe women are nurturing and emotional but men are visual. They think so differently than women. A few selective men study the essence of a woman to understand her. Likewise, selective women study the essence and nature of a man to understand his rhythm. Gaining a general understanding a male is helpful but understanding the individual male in a marriage I believe requires prerequisite knowledge. Each husband married to each wife is a personal individual case to understand. His entire life's journey is associated with him, and his intellect defines him. His spiritual relationship with God seals him. My plans are to allow my husband to be the man, and I will accept him for being true to himself. One thing for sure, I will make sure we maintain and manage effective open communication, even if we have to write notes, and journals to see our way out of storms.

We will be talking things over. Without an open door to communicate, we have no union. In a marriage, anything may happen and hopefully true love and a prayerful marriage will help manage the unity of the marriage according to. Just from watching couples from a little girl, a marriage is an institution, and the husband is the CFO, and God is the CEO. The wife is the help meet. She is the nurturing force that is tuned into the intricate parts of the marriage. Her body is designed with a womb that can develop and carry life inside while nurturing and preparing to give birth. We are a massive creation able to produce life. The man is the life producer is he responsible for housing the main ingredient to initiate the conception of life. He is a protector that covers his family. The situation with the bank officer is another reason to surround yourself with godly friends who will not violate such a moment. I saw enough growing up to make sure when I do marry to maintain and manage my married appropriately. It will take too so providing I should marry. I believe I am finally prepared to marry. I will not be looking like a beauty queen every time my husband sees me around the house, but I will be pretty close.

He will see my hair in a ponytail and up in a ponytail or all over my head. The next day I may be looking regal and royal the next, but if I can help it. He will not see me hit rock bottom wearing to warn our robes and other warn our essentials. He will see a bathroom filled with fine French soap and especially mango. I know for sure I hope to own an estate with a master suite with his and hers complete private bathrooms. Personally, I think that easier on the marriage. Vital are the the early merging years shared between two people becoming one. I hope not to take being relaxed around my husband to the extreme but to maintain the rhythm of dating while married. The bank office obviously is one of the impeccable style and taste for the finer things. He was holding a ticking mental time bomb concerning his wife. He was working in the midst of well-kept attractive women at work, while his wife being her natural self feeling relaxed around her husband clueless that he was fed up with the way she was looking. At least, he mentioned nothing about her weight, and hopefully she is maintaining her weight because he might have a problem with additional pounds. Home is the place where you are supposed to relax and let your hair down. Knowing my husband I am sure will go beyond open communications, it is what he may not communicate. The silent words are the problem. I am glad I allowed the bank officer to release all his frustrations concerning his wife. It helped to see inside the mind of a man when he is not speaking what is in his heart. Grateful to Dr. Ocho for allowing me to attend the marriage seminar while I was single. I had a chance to use empathy and sow a blessing. When I should marry and my husband, for some reason, becomes silently and privately disgusted with me opening his mouth to talk about me to someone. I pray I reap what I sowed into the marriage of the bank office and his wife. I did not ask how long they had been married, but I knew not to invade the marriage but to help. When he finished releasing his frustrations, I asked him another question, "Are you able to go shopping for lunch at a couple of fine stores?" He answered, saying, "Yes." I advised him to take notes."

Early the next morning I received another telephone call, as soon as I took my seat to start work. The caller was a female, and she was crying uncontrollably. It was difficult trying to understand her words. "Calm down so I can understand what you are saying." She continued to cry harder. "I am here and I want to understand what you are saying so calm down so I may help you." "Thank you so much," she said. Then she started crying again. "I am listening, thank me for what?" She cried some more and finally, I held the phone so she could collect herself to share the rest of the "Thank you." "My husband is a tall handsome man, and any other women would have willingly destroyed my marriage. He told me what happened and all the things you told him to do for me. I came home and he had so many beautiful things laid out on the bed and in the bathroom were so many fancy French soaps, and expensive perfumes." She broke down crying again, saying, "Thank you," between each breath she could manage.

Now, I was about to cry with her. Her husband took control of the telephone saying, "Hi. I shared everything with her. I told her about my telephone call to you yesterday morning, while at work. I told her everything you advised me to do for her." I was about to lose it, my tears were pressing and begging for a release out of prison. He said, "Thank you, thank you for everything. " "God bless the both of you." I replied. We hung up the telephone, and finally my restrained tears were granted permission of freedom. I was in a tall cubicle so no one could see me crying. At that moment, I was so thankful to God that I attended that marriage seminar.

Noticing, they both missed work calling me from home, whereas they both must have taken a day of vacation to celebrate another level in their marriage. All the glory belongs to God but this is I desire to be used of God–to cause a change at the right moment. The amazing revelation, attending the marriage seminar allowed me to see marriage couples together. They were on display sharing the bridges they were trying to cross. The information was personal but I knew the importance of maintaining confidentiality. Eventually, I for both their names. The first thing the husband mentioned was his frustration with the old robes and holes in her leisure clothing. Perhaps I may be privileged to attend another marriage seminar concerning. How comfortable is comfortable?

Becoming one is an area I hope to learn more about before I marry. My husband will be the head of our home as Christ is his head, and Christ the head of Christ. Above all, I will have no concerns, hesitations, or problems surrendering and being submissive to my future husband.

As a submissive emanated wife I pray to be an effective help meet. Maintaining and managing a gentle disposition as a woman of God. Making sure I include in the bridal registry beautiful French soaps and gift certificates for stylish Victorian robes, matching house slippers with two inch heels, beautiful bath robes, leisure robes, and fine perfumes. Likewise, include the same essential for my future husband. Hoping to maintain and manage an effective time for effective communication.

Hypothetically, I believe God allowed me to meet Robert because I was reaping seeds which I had sown, into that marriage. Not knowing all the details and how many times or if that was the gentleman's first attempt to date outside of his marriage, which I believe it was his first attempt because he was frustrated.

People must have prayed for their marriage. Amazing how God's spiritual clock was working covering an ordained marriage. He called the right person at the right time. The difference between the singles' ministry and the marriage seminar was being able to see the real couple to look into their eyes. I heard the actual difficulties, which they shared. It helped me to respect the covenant marriage and never violate their vows even when they are willing and seeking to break their own sealed vows. I refused to be a participant. It was meant for me to attend the marriage seminar. Dr. Ocho addressed the heart of a marriage shared between a man and a woman. I walked away from the seminar thinking of a marriage as honorable and marriage is to be respected at all cost. Life changes and people change with life experience either negatively or positively. I pray to grow with my potential husband as he and I change. I want to learn about his change and grow with him. After all, we will be as one. The heart of the matter Dr. Ocho stressed were empathy, but empathy required effective communication between a husband and wife.

What I witnessed with the married couples was a plethora of vital information. When Dr. Ocho instructed one couple to a role pray by holding hands looking through each other in the eye-it was every effective. Thinking of a spiritual transfusion to know how the person was feeling. Attending the seminar helped me to do the right thing turning a husband's attention back to the attention of his covenant marriage.

I am glad the call was made to me, and I am thankful for Dr. Ocho allowing me as a single woman to attend the seminar. I have always desired to be married to my own husband and knowing I hope the woman my husband reached out to would send my husband back to me. I did for her what I hope to reap in my own marriage, if my husband should omit talking with me about our marriage. I do not remember his name or the name of his wife, but I remember the incident. One morning I woke up thinking about reaping and this moment of history came to my thoughts. Furthermore, I appreciate, respect, and understand the covenant marriage.

Be not deceived; God is not mocked: for whatsoever a man soweth, that shall he also reap. Galatians 6:7 [KJV]

Wherefore they are no more twain, but one flesh. What therefore God hath joined together, let not man put asunder. Matthew 19:6 [KJV]

I was about to encounter the audible voice of God, and Robert

Robert pulled four car links in front of me. It took time for
him to reduce his speed after I pulled over to the shoulder

SEPTEMBER 1995

While driving from Mesquite, Texas ending a fairly new relationship, which was not conducive for a healthy relationship, which God had not planned for me. What felt painfully disappointing at a time was really a moment to celebrate. On the night before meeting Robert, I received a telephone call from a lady sharing with me a warning concerning the person I thought I knew was not the person for me. She was braved and sincere enough to express a truth to me. Thanking her for the information I prepared for bed and woke up earlier than usual allowing travel time to Mesquite, Texas knowing I had an early morning appointment with my professional printer to go over the details for the flyers and programs. I was featured two twins male models formerly models from a major publication company. My name, boutique, and reputation were in the spotlight.

The number one African American Radio Station and high profile radio personalities were involved, and I rode the wave to raise scholarship funds for my alma mater over the radio. I was running myself tired, but I enjoyed being busy meeting new people every single day. If that lady had never made that telephone call the night before, I may have never met Robert, while driving upon the freeway. I trusted her words because of her approach, and she was happily married. Facing the truth is better than hearsay, and I am glad she made that call, whereas it was the catalysts that led me to be in the appointed location.

What I did not know, God revealed. It's so easy to waste precious time being involved in a non-conducive relationship, which was fairly new. Participating in a subtle relationship with a hidden agenda and secret motives unaware is a reason to pray and ask God to reveal what is hidden. Sometimes when friends and relatives refuse to listen to the truth prayer is essential. A man of street smarts may quickly spot a naïve sheltered female because a street sharp woman will wreck his day, so he sets his prey for the unlearned. Honestly, I knew nothing about the streets or the games, but I knew how to pray. What happened on Stemmons Freeway, in September 1995, I thought was dead and buried for 15 years. Even so, God reminded me of His spoken words on January 16, 2011:

So shall my word be that goeth forth out of my mouth: it shall not return unto me void, but it shall accomplish that which I please, and it shall prosper in the thing whereto I sent it. Isaiah 55:11[KJV]

Preparation, process, and development of God's spoken words always cause a shake before the shift for the manifestation. Attacks validate his spoken words! I decided to make an Inquiry of Joseph, the dream, the son of Jesses [read his story, in the bible] Through these past 40 years, I have managed with God on my side to master aggressive attacks and insults from fake friends, hostile people, people with mental imbalances, which was hidden], deceptive people, abuse, abusive people, torment, jealously, deadly attacks, and intimidation in the spirit of appreciation. Attending college as an adult is a challenge but God's spiritual classroom I discovered consist of trails and tribulations. People not only make the round go round, but they empower you with spiritual strength to endure and grow up with a made up mind to serve God.

People come and people go so I am able to convert every negative towards a positive by applying the **heart** of Romans 8:28. There is a heart in Romans 8:28. My mind is made-up to serve God! This is the only way I will earn the spiritual grade of an A. I had to realize that God is on my side even when a spoken promise takes fifteen years or longer to manifest.

Smiles came easy to my face because my smiles were like garments-I changed into each day. I knew how to wear a smile to cover the pain, and the tears. Laughing served as the accessories to adorn the smile to make sure the pain was hidden.

Thankful to God, I too had a praying a grandmother named Millie Annie Mitchell [a.k.a., Big Mama], and a great grandmother [her one and only daughter Fannie Banks Franklin] with the weekly company of an additional twelve female senior citizen that nurtured me in prayer as a very tiny girl. Without knowing or thinking about the future, God knew to grind me in prayer. When my Big Mama passed away, I prayed so many days never realizing that God knew what I would need to survive. Sometimes Big Mama would look deep into my eyes, as if she could see things beyond the current time. God employed my grannies and those twelve little white haired ladies to prepare before me a Table of Prayer. These ladies nursed and nurtured me in prayer, and they were sold-out to God saints. I call them my godly wisdom saints. They walked the walk of righteousness, and their lifestyles were in the likeness of Christ.

The man, in the spotlight had so many secrets that were known by other people but hid in the dark from me. God had better plans, which was my "Ram in the Bush," experience. The young lady telephone to speak a truth to me, which led me to take the long drive to Mesquite, Texas, whereas, I was later driving on the freeway heading the opposite direction southward, which in actuality was the right appointed path to be in view for Robert. There are so many questions I desire to ask Robert concerning the start of his military life, and when did he first notice me on, or before I drove upon to Stemmons Freeway.

Life was so busy when I met him, and he was full of conversation, and I never had the chance to talk to him because I was listening to him. If he woke me up at 1am, 2am, 3am, while traveling, I knew it was required of me to listen to him and give him my undivided attention. Which means, many times I had to wake up to be alert. Everything about Robert was different, and I acknowledge as an attentive gentleman. It was better than he called me and wake me up, versus him finding another woman on the streets. Being in the position to wake up and listen, it was my pleasure to listen to Robert talk. When he called me being so far away it meant he was thinking about me, so I honored him with my full attention.

When I moved home at the end of November 1995, he continued to call me during the early morning hours, which continued when I started working as a contract temporary assignments before returning to the bank full time. I woke up at 5:30am to prepare and catch the first bus to the train station because I did not have the extra cash for gas nor to park downtown. Riding the bus and the train provided me the time to read books, and walking provided me the exercise I needed for physical fitness.

I had just finished praying about the situation before she called me, and I never revealed her, but I thanked her. She was a happily married woman. I met her once, and she shared with me on that night, "He is wrong for you." Knowing when to listen and when to reject helped me to walk right into a blessing. Deep down, I prepared myself to see the truth as I turned the corner inside the apartment complex, I saw his vehicle parked. Pulling up next to his vehicle, I left him a note to let him know I knew the truth. Touching his car, it was cold, which meant he spent the night. Preparing to leave, I blew my car horn quickly knowing he would check his vehicle. When he opened the door, he knew it was over. There was no way for me to know except someone close sharing his secrets. Surely, he wondered how I knew that was the look on his face. They reminded me to be mindful never to mention the name of the person but act.

The act is what concerns God. Sin against brothers and sisters, in the gospel are committed with an act, flesh and blood is the covering, which is why we are often deceived as a victim, or we deceive others by hiding the truth. When a person repented of their sins or sin, we may not be aware, and if we call up the sin and attach it to the name of the person, we stand to be in violation with God. Therefore, being careful not to walk into an offense:

He will turn again, he will have compassion upon us; he will subdue our iniquities; and wilt cast all their sings into the depths of the sea. Micah 7:19[KJV]

Feeling free, I drove off quietly as he was standing in the door looking as if he had lost his best friend. There was not much he could say to savage the relationship, and it felt right seeing with my own eyes. A surprise encounter prevented me from being entangled in a web of deception. When people speak it sounds as if they are telling the truth since words spoken, written, and announced are powerful. Growing up sheltered and not having knowledge of the street was another reason to pray. Therefore, what I was not able to see; God was watching and listening on my behalf. There was so much to learn about relationships, mental behavior, backgrounds, motives, family history, and the history of the person behavior.

The only lesson I was given in regard to dating came from my Big Mama, when I was about eight years of age. She asked me to pull up a chair close to the side of her bed. She had fallen and broken her hip on the front porch. Each day after school, I would stop by and comb her hair, give her a bed bath, and rub her feet with oil. I pulled up my chair close to her bed, and she said, "Ninnie, you cannot trust every man. They are not all honest." As I sat in that chair looking at my granny, I said, "Yes, Ma is." She looked into straight into my eyes probably knowing that I had no idea what she was talking about. Perhaps her spoken words were seeds for a later harvest of information. Everyone knew my father did not allow me to date anyone so My Big Mama was the only person that spoke to me concerning dating, but I was too young to understand the message.

Obviously, her spoken words of advice must have taken root and God waters because when it comes to dating a man what I do not trust I discard and separate without delay. As I was driving down the freeway to my appointment to meet the printer with the layout, pictures, and graphs for the program, I thought to pull over and call him officially ending the relationship. Making the call was easy and all I said, was, "You know it's over and forget about me." I hung up the telephone leaving him without the opportunity to tell a lie to cover up a lie. I stepped back into my vehicle driving southward on the freeway. Remembering the musical tape, which was recorded and clued the night before I pushed the tape in order to hear the music for the models making sure each transition from one song to the next was smooth and clear. Boney James was the first song on the track, which was to be played as the people came into the auditorium.

The instructions were typed and ready for the technician to transfer the music into the main school system. As soon as I turned up the volume, I heard the audible voice of the LORD speaking, saying, He is your husband. I slammed my breaks. The time was around 10:30am, which the traffic was with on a few cars ahead of me and others not in my lane. The Holy Spirit knows when to speak. I turned to take a look into my backseat thinking maybe someone was hiding in the back seat of my vehicle during the time I stopped using the pay telephone.

Not seeing anyone, I realized the words were spoken from the audible voice of the LORD, so I pressed the gas pedal to regain my speed turning to the right to face the front and much to my surprise. There was this tall gentleman over to my right riding side-by-side trying to get my attention. I was speeding because I was running late. He was aggressively beckoning for me to pull over. In my mind, I was trying to decipher the words spoken from the audible voice, and while looking at the terribly handsome man to my right, which I was preparing to pull over to the shoulder of the freeway and go completely off. My thoughts were focused passed insults and violations I was about to miss a future blessing. Within a moment, here comes another blessing. I looked at Robert again, and said, "God, I know you are not talking about that man I just cut loose from my life."

Robert was bold, strong-willed, and aggressively beckoning for me to pull over. Finally, I pulled over because the audible voice had spoken. It took me a minute to slow down on the shoulder because my speed was far above sixty five miles. The gentleman driving the brand new Cadillac took a minute to pull over because of his speed trying to keep up with me. I was rehearsing words to go off because I was loaded with verbiage from the mental luggage from the previous relationship I had currently ended. Watching intently as his car door opened and out came his long athletic legs. I noticed the coordination of his designer shoes, slacks, shirt, and his authoritative walk. I started thinking it might not be at my best interest to go off.

There was something all together different about this gentleman. A certain peace came over me, while the spoken words from the audible voice continued to visit my thoughts, He is your husband. Everything ugly and mean words I thought to speak left me instantly. This gentle was so tall, slender, and athletically fit completely. Surely, he must have known how handsome he was with all that confidence.

Standing at my car window on the driver's side, I let the window down halfway, in case I decided to go off. The first words he spoke, "I must apologize for that scene on the freeway." I smiled, responding, "No problem." In the back of my mind, I was saying, "If you only knew what I was thinking earlier." A handsome, well-dressed man will catch my eye, but it is difficult to grab and capture my attention. He said, "My name is Robert." "Linda is my name." He said, "It's a pleasure to meet you." I replied, "Likewise." We talked about my fashion show project, and I shared with him that I was busy and exhausted. He asked if he could call me, and I passed him my business card, and he in turn passed me his card with a number to reach him all over the world, plus an additional number. He desired to attend the show but his travel engagement prevented the pleasure of his presence.

Robert then asked me of my plans after the show, so we could get together and talk. I expressed to him that as soon as the ends I would be making plans to travel to Hawaii. "May I asked how many will be in your company," asked Robert? "Just me." I replied. Looking down into my eyes, with a soft gentle caring voice he said, "I am in the military, and I have been stationed in Hawaii twice and Hawaii is not the place for a lady to travel alone. If you don't mind waiting until after I complete my travel, I will accompany you to Hawaii to protect you. The entire expense of the airline tickets and expenses are on me." Instead of being excited, I experienced a flash back from the mental luggage of the last case of a man.

Looking up at him with a ready mouth to go off but my tongue was bridled again, thinking of the words spoken by the audible voice, He is your husband. I smiled and said, "Sure, that's nice of you." Knowing if I remained in that position with him, I might say the wrong thing, so I expressed to him that I was running late to my appointment. He said, "I will call you very soon." He bent down and kissed me on my forehead, and I nearly melted. His aura was powerful and I had never felt such an aura from any man on that magnitude. Roberts's aura was like a 7.0 the Richter monitoring an earthquake, which meeting he felt like an earthquake shook up my life.

As Robert walked away from my vehicle my eyes were focused on the man inside, there was more to Robert than with an average man.

He was far beyond your average man by all means. He walked away from my vehicle leaving me mesmerized. The most intriguing man I have ever met, in my life. Managing to pull myself together to drive back on to the freeway, passing him. I waved, and he waved back. My mind was left behind on that spot on the freeway with Robert. I drove to the printer in another zone. Amazing how everything changed in a matter of minutes. Robert meant more to me than anyone I had ever met in my life. I entertained sharing with him the words spoken by the audible voice, but I held those words for another time. Not knowing his spiritual level I waited.

Arriving at to meet with my professional printer. I was there but my mind was far away with Robert and on the freeway. His aura was all around me, as if we had transformed into each other. When I think back, on that special day I am reminded of God's provisions for our lives, which takes me straight with the situation with Jonah:

Now the LORD had prepared a great fish to swallow up Jonah. And Jonah was in the belly of the fish three days and three nights. Jonah 1:17 [KJV]

Understanding the thoughts and ways of God are higher than my ways:

For my thoughts are not your thoughts, neither are your ways my ways, saith the LORD. For as the heavens are higher than the earth, so are my ways higher than your ways, and my thoughts than your thoughts. Isaiah 55:8-9 [KJV]

Therefore, this passage in the Bible leads me directly to *Jeremiah 29:11 [KJV]*:

For I know the thoughts that I think toward you, saith the LORD, thoughts of peace, and not of evil to give you an expected end.

The comfort and peace of reading, trusting, and understanding the word of God is the compass, which I need to guide me continuously. Writing about the experience of the four words spoken by the audible voice of God, HE IS YOUR HUSBAND, and meeting Robert at that moment brings me to the situation concerning Elijah and the widow woman:

And the word of the LORD came unto him, saying, Arise, get thee to Zarephath, which belongeth to Zidon, and dwell there: behold, I have commanded a widow woman there to sustain thee. So he arose and went to Zarephath. And when he came to the gate of the city, behold, the widow woman was there gathering of sticks: and he called to her, and said, Fetch me, I pray thee, a little water in a vessel, that I may drink. 1 Kings 17: 8-10 [KJV].

When God speaks to you either by his small still voice, audible voice, and or the unction [anointing] of the Holy Spirit, which is mentioned in *1 John 2:20 [KJV]:*

But ye have unction from the Holy One, and ye know all things.

You become aggressive, determined, and fueled with a force to accomplish His instructions. Elijah moved into action accordingly traveling to Zarephath, as he was instructed by the LORD. When the LORD speaks a word, His word will bring results. You may have to wait for it, and it may tarry [linger]:

For the vision is yet for an appointed time, but at the end it shall speak, and not lie: though it tarry, wait for it; because it will surely come, it will not tarry. Habakkuk 2:3 [KJV]

So many Biblical Verses come to mind in relations to waiting on the fruition and manifestation of a word from the LORD and the story surrounding Noah and the ark is a prime example of the validity of God's spoken word. When God speaks, something will happen. His word is a conception. It will start to develop, process, and prepare for the performance.

THE PRINT SHOP

$\mathcal{T}$he moment I arrived at my printer's place of business, in Desoto, Texas, she asked me several times if I was focused on the meeting, which she continued asking me if I was focused because I was undoubtedly in a mesmerized daze. I pondered the experience to keep the moment fresh because normally when you share an experience of hearing the audible voice of God, and meeting a gentleman person listening to often destroy the joy with negative words. Eventually, deciding not to take the risk, I was lost in memory of the gentleman from the freeway. It felt as if a God set the engagement of the marriage on the freeway.

No engagement ring was placed on my finger, but the spirit of engagement was flowing in my spirit. In the short twenty minutes or we spoke on the shoulder of the freeway. I was treated like a lady of distinction and personally. I had never felt that way before. An abundance of calmness rushed over me as I embraced the kindness of his disposition and spoken words. His mannerism was so gentle compared to his aggressive approach trying to get my attention as I was driving extremely fast. My printers were great people, but I pondered my thoughts desiring to feast on the joy of meeting a gentleman. Easily recognized, I was in a mesmerized moment saturated with thoughts of the freeway encounter of hearing the audible voice of God, and meeting Robert. His spirit was invading my thoughts, as if he were standing beside me at the shop.

Meeting new people all the time and never experiencing the unthinkable of meeting Robert on the freeway. I wondered if I had never looked over to my right would I have missed the opportunity. Surely, Robert may have followed with a second plan being an aviation pilot. A pilot must think of quick solutions. He was a true gentleman by nature. I was not able to shake the thoughts of Robert Mentally, his presence lingered with me continuously. Participating in the meeting was like being physically present but my mind was so far away. Trying to keep my focus on business but Robert interrupted my life, in a good way. Those four audible words spoken by the voice of God was dancing in my thoughts. There was no time to stop and journal the information but I was having a nice celebration of what felt like a fresh new beginning.

Meeting Robert woke up all my happy senses. Being in a joyful state being busy with the project was fulfilling alone. The joy of meeting so many people and planning for a successful event was flowing with a rhythm, harmony, and creating a melody, in my life. The collage of private thoughts was in celebration mode pondering the essence of meeting Robert, and hearing the audible voice from God. Meeting a meticulous and distinctive debonair gentleman increased my joy, and I felt as if I was floating on a cloud of splendor. Robert was now residing, in my space, my movement, and with me, in my journey. He was planted in my life by God, and I knew he would be there for a long time. I held Robert deep in my heart but the words spoken by the audible voice of God saturated my soul, and I merged with his spirit.

Finding the right words to express what I experienced to do not exist but becoming one with a man is what happened on that designated day, September 1995. His spirit filtrated moving into my spirit, and I was no longer an unmarried wife but I became Robert's chosen wife from God. God sealed, protected, the private sacred garden he planted to grow in true love. Realizing the book had to be written to give God glory across the globe. For years, I pondered that day and hoping to see Robert again. I have never been mesmerized by a man until that day on the freeway. God stopped time and made time for me to meet Robert at his appointed time.

The element of surprise is always a lasting memory because there was no plan, motive, or secret agenda, but it just happened. I keep seeing him walking towards me on the freeway. Always remembering and never forgetting the style of his authoritative walk, which he captured me as he was walking to me. If I could replay that moment, in time with a cell phone camera, I might have pretended to be talking to someone but snapping picture after the picture. And if I knew I was going to meet such a man, I would have turned on the mini recorder to forever enjoy this spoken words, which he gave me a cassette on the last day I saw him, and I never had the chance to listen all the way through. If I could one day find that black cassette tape, I am sure it was more than the sound of him training for flight. I met Robert, when life was busy and later turned upside down.

Many days I started listening to the recording but all I could hear was loud noise, so I felt that would be consistent all the way through. A roaring sound of a jet engine and men instructing Robert of new features is what I thought I would hear throughout. Nevertheless, something tells me there was more, in the middle and at the end. Robert, I believe had recorded a personal message to me. I would only listen to one minute, and I stopped the recording but I held on to the tape until one day. It came up missing.

As we engaged in a conversation concerning women, and he said, "Linda, I do not have a problem with women." His words shot through me as a reminder to protect my heart because he is a pilot, handsome, wealthy, and he is in the military. He spoke what I never wanted to hear out of his mouth. The words he spoke sounded so familiar reminding me of a deceptive man with the joy of women flooding his life. I may have misunderstood his intended message, and I repent of that moment. At which point, I started blocking my interest to protect my heart, which was a mistake. I was carrying old mental luggage, while speaking to a God sent gentleman.

Actually, he looked at me puzzled not realizing that he snapped a cord, in me. I raised my voice to him for the first time saying, "I did not ask you all of that." He said, "Well, all I am trying to say, is I do not have a problem with women." My response the second time was sharper, saying, "I do not having a problem with men either. You are wealthy, tall, handsome, physically fit, sing like an angel, and a military pilot what women, in their right mind would pass you up Robert?." He looked at me with that authoritative stare, as if he was saying, "Woman do not raise your voice to me." I clocked the look because his demeanor changed with firmness. Not completely knowing his character, and I was facing a deficiency concerning a military officer. I thought it be best to respond delicately so I lowered my voice acknowledging his transformed countenance.

Experiencing flashback moments of being feisty and checking a man, I was in the presence of a different kind of man. He was an military officer, and I flipped a switch because Robert did most of the talking. He is an effective communicator, and I enjoyed listening to his spoken words. Robert was trying to convey a message that he was picky and not any woman would do for him. He desired a special woman of character and style, a woman who loved him for him. However, I guess I was entitled to one moment of igorance. Communication absent of empathy is unhealthy for me. Listening and carefully examining the unspoken meaning before responding was a challenge. Talking to a military officer is no comparison to a man lacking structure and discipline.

I had so much to learn about a real man. I went into myself thinking of the relationship, I had just ended mixing those elements with something fresh and unique from God required the help of the Holy Spirit. New territory is a reason to think before speaking. Sealing my heart because I was deep into Robert, and I mean completely saturated. He was the man who God announced as my husband. However, there was so much for me to learn about relating to a real man. A man who knows he is a man, a military officer. His confidence and caliber were obvious that he was a different breed. Those days of going off and clocking a man ended with Robert. I knew that he would not tolerate a disruptive form of communication. He set a standard for the expected tone. He is strong, authoritative, and aggressive, and he took control of a situation. I would scream and go off on most men, especially when they got on my nerves or say something totally stupid but Robert was not afraid of me. He knew how to give me that look, saying, "That will not be tolerated." I understood the look. Knowing from the first meeting, he was willing to protect and cover me, I was willing to be submissive.

My emotions were scattered but I knew there was something profound about Robert. I knew he was my husband but there was an internal wrestlet to guard my heart just in case. God separated us for 15 years for whatever reason.

Robert swept me off my feet, which meant he had me in place to rule me leading me as a submissive emanated wife. Most of the time Robert did all the talking, and I listened intently. It was a joy listening to him talk. There was a moment, while in Roberts company, it was urgently necessary for me to retreat to the powder room, and he asked, "Do you have to go now?" I was in a tight. I thought to myself, "Is he self-centered and ridiculous or what?" Without yelling as I did before, I employed a gentle voice, saying, "I cannot hold it, I really need to go." I went, and while out of his sight, I pondered thoughts about the side of him, I did not know. . "Robert requires closeness, and he will guard your time with value. He might have a touch of possessiveness. He is not willing to share his wife with anyone and especially her time. It all belongs to him to treasure and enjoy. Things are in seemingly, in harmony on his terms." Returning to his presence, he was fine and his conversation returned to full volume. He always held my hand seeking intimate closeness of being knitted together and never divided.

An abundance of protective characteristics with an affectionate and sentimental nature made it easy to think and ponder about Robert. People have a way of speaking and inflicting their misery on top of your joy, so I made a decision to mediate on Robert. Remembering the evening of the day I met Robert on the freeway. I finally finished running all over town and head home to relax taking a nap. Later that night, the telephone rang, and it was Robert. My heart started to beat really fast. My thoughts entertained so many questions to ask Robert, but with.

Him being an effective communicator with so much to share listening to his heart was my pleasure. Enjoying the sound of his voice and respecting that he was traveling. I honored his need to communicate without interrupting. Each time he called. I listened to Robert sharing his daily activities with me. We talked every day, and he did most of the talking.

Every time he called. I listened to his words intently. Then the call came from Robert, saying, "I am in your state, give me the directions to your condominium." Upon his arrival I came outside since it was the first meeting to my place of residence being a female. The moment I walked close to him and took a seat. he greeted me with a kiss on my forehead and took control of my left hand. He held my hand the entire time as he opened his heart to me sharing his life more intimately. Seated at the park talking beyond eight hours, he never released my hand, not once. In so many ways, the moment felt like a blood transfusion. Robert's spirit was flowing and my spirit was meeting and agreeing with his spirit harmoniously. I remember feeling the abundance of peace, comfort, and delight being so close to Robert, and listening to the soothing sound of his masculine voice. Detecting Robert was a sacred man set apart from the rest was easy.

During the entire time he was talking, I got to know the other side of Robert, which most women never wait for and accept. It was the tender, gentle, loving side, which is to be nurtured delicately with listening ears. His character and essence were phenomenal, which was first announced by his prodigious aura from the inner man. Accepting his words as he spoke from his heart. he allowed me the opportunity to accept him for Robert. I embraced his vulnerability because in the beginning, I embraced his boldness, strength, authority, and intelligence. Making sure I closed his communication with kindness, I never broke my hand free from him until he released his grip to free my hand.

When you love, you will naturally cover, seal, and protect that which is private. No matter how angry a man may cause you to respond, what you sealed is protected beyond the anger and any other acts. When God closed the flesh of active, he never reopened his flesh, but he spoke to his spirit. As so when, God caused a deep sleep to fall upon Adam, and he slept: and he took one of his ribs, and closed up the flesh instead thereof [Adam was vulnerable but God covered him]; And the rib, which the LORD God had taken from man, made he a woman, and brought her unto the man [Genesis 2:21-22 KJV]. Adam made an identity of the woman, saying. This is now bone of my bones, and flesh of my flesh: she shall be called Woman, because she was taken out of Man [Genesis 2:23 KJV].

A women's intuition helped me to never interrupted his time of communication, and I will never interrupt him because I have learned before I met Robert and Pastor Jakes He advised and I am paraphrasing his spoken words, which he spoke to the ladies of the congregation to "never ever violate a man, when he opens his heart to you. Even if you make you angry, please do not violate the opening of a man's heart. If you violate him, he will close his heart and it will become difficult for him to open up to you again." Near the end of Robert's communication, whereas he was he opening his heart tome, he turned to face me saying, "When I saw you driving on the freeway, "**I know you are my wife.**" He paused and said, again, "I know you are my wife." I am here holding your hand, and **I know you are my wife.**" **Eventually, I pulled over and what a journey to embrace and endure. He came to visit me since the first time we met on the freeway about six or seven days later during our second visit, "I knew when I saw you driving on the freeway, you were my wife."We met in September1995, and he was deployed to Bosnia at the end of December 1995. I assumed he was shot down in Bosnia. I lost all the information he gave me, when I moved twice. I forgot his last name. I dreamed of him after fifteen years fifteen years of silent dreams. He spoke to me for the first time, in the dream on January 16, 2011.**

The words spoken from the audible voice returned to visit me again to confirm his spoken words, but I pondered the words not feeling comfortable. I enjoyed being spent those amazing quality hours with Robert, but I knew the hour was getting late, and it was time for me to go inside. We talked for about another hour because I desired for his communication to simmer, settle, relax and seal before I separated from him. Understanding, the open heart of a man, it is important to allow his heart to close.

Obviously, Robert had to be a caliber man for God to point me into his direction. If God had never spoken, I may have missed Robert, well, I sense unequivocally, he would have found **a** way to get my attention. After all Robert and I were in a spiritual rhythm, and God's purpose would be settled that day. It was my desire to embrace and protect his quality time of communications while holding my hand. When I met him, I embraced his strength on the freeway, and when he held my left hand, I embraced him as I plan for the rest of my life. He is by no means a weak man, but he is all man, the kind of man who God planted in this world for me to love, nurture, respect, and honor. I waited for his words to be sealed and protected because they were tender, and it was my position to cover his open heart until he returned to his authoritative position.

God opened Robert's heart, that I may understand the nature of a real man. A real man determined to pursue the one and only lady of his interest. A man may appear tough and rough on the outside that is his protective shield. A man is first human, and he is not superman. Experiencing a husband's strength and vulnerable nature together, and at different times is the duties of a help meet, and wife. He is not to be judge but understood. Understanding your husband requires godly wisdom by knowing the power of a help meet, which is to cover and protect her man never exposing to others the condition of his heart under any circumstances. A help meet stands by her husband, and she builds him up. She is his personal psychologist under the covenant of marriage. Likewise, when a husband and wife are intimate, in the bedroom it is private because the bedroom of the couple married to each other, the bedroom is not defiled.

Discussing private intimate matters of the bedroom plants a vivid picture of your private intimate life, in the minds of others. Outside people have no place in your bedroom. A private intimate marriage will only grow because the prize of the two joined together as one will elevate together forever. Seeing that Robert, transfers to his masculine strength, I expressed to him, it was time for me to head inside. He looked into my eyes and asked me if he could sing to me. Thinking to myself as we stood face-to-face "He'd better not sound terrible," because I will tell him the truth. As I was standing in front of Robert waiting for him to open his mouth to sing, he was looking down into my eyes and the moment I started to smile at him. He opened his mouth and started singing sounding like a hosts of angels from around the throne.

I tried my best not to cry but all the wells of tears were forming preparing to salute the voice of a powerful man standing before me. Hearing the sound of his voice, felt like a million butterflies rushing inside my soul preparing to flay their wings and fly. My heart was already beating remembering the audible voice of God resonating, saying. He is your husband. It was such an amazing moment where I nearly fainted.

He was singing a gospel song with ease and with the anointing. His voice ministered to me under the light of the moon one special night. When he finished singing, I asked him to explain, and he said, "I sang with a professional gospel group." He called out the name of the group, but I forgot. I said to him, "You are awesome singing by yourself." I stood there in silence looking into his eyes wandering and desiring if the moment was right to share with him what God had spoken in my car as I was driving on the freeway. I love looking into Robert's eyes.

Peace and truth reflected in his eyes, if felt as if I was looking into his soul, deep into his soul where I had transferred. Right from the start, I trusted Robert. There was no hesitation with trusting him. I wanted to stand there forever and never walk away from him. We stood there for the longest looking into each other's eyes with silence. I hugged him to seal the night of intimacy from the heart. He kissed me on my forehead and I turned to head back to my condominium.

It was difficult walking away from the man name Robert. He came back the next day, which was Saturday, and we went for a long ride, which I believe may have been the eight day. There is something special about the eight day, whereas it felt as if I had known Robert all my life. He felt right and he felt peaceful, and my life was relaxed, in his presence.

Subsequently, he was talking the whole time but the contents of his communication were perfectly timed. At each pause, I thought to express a few things to him, but before I could open my mouth, he continued to talk. I knew if I married him most of my writing would be during his deployment or while he was taken a nap. Gathering he may acquire my undivided attention without distractions. Everything he talked about was so interesting and exciting. I enjoyed being in his company so very much because Robert is authoritative and in-charge kind of gentleman. Sometimes I would call Robert, and he would always call me, and sometimes he would call and wake me up early in the wee mornings, so he could talk. It was fine with me, because I would wake up and talk to him for as long as he desired to talk, even if I was sleepy. I wanted him to know I was at home alone, and that he could call me anytime. He got busy with travel, but we yet talked and I moved home after the show, and I moved again.

The second time I met with Robert, was at this park, which is
also the place where he held my left hand for over eight hours
sharing his heart with tears gently running down his cheeks

THE POWER OF HOLDING HANDS

*L*earning the results of tender affection from holding hands started; with my first experience of feeding three white rabbits happened when my father stopped off, in Longview, Texas to introduce us to additional kinfolks. Her name was Ola but they called her Cousin Puttin. She was extremely fair, and so was her grandson, which he stood at the time 6 feet 2, and he was only a few years older than me. It was my first visit to East, Texas, and I was not a happy camper. The raw country life was a SHOCK! I was experienced in a little amount of living in a country setting, but I was not prepared for this level of a country living with; well water, outback house, no bathtub, no running water, no street lights, a party line, and cows. Everthing was differnt. People kissed you all over your face, while holding your face.

The first time I visited the country, I spent most of the time stooping the ground and having a temper tantrum. My father just laughed instead of knocking the fire out of my madness. I spent so much time running from what I called black wasp, they called them something else. My father kept laughing and would not stop, which made me that much angrier. I wanted to go back to the city. Then mother Ardie [respectfully called Muh] prepared breakfast, lunch, and dinner with the wood burning stove. I could not believe my eyes–I was about to be sick to my stomach as life was happening outside of the box, which I was familiar. As I was walking outside near the front gate, in time to catch my father running from the outhouse with his pants down. A snake met him, right in the middle of his lavatory business. He was running and laughing, realizing the obvious; I started laughing, which broke the temperature of my anger. He spent the day laughing at me, and the time switched so I could laugh at him. It was a very funny moment, whereas from that moment forward the ice in me started to relax and accept the rawness of a country.

Heading back to Dallas, Texas, was always with a stop in Longview, to visit Cousin Puttin, and her grandson. I will refer to him as Charlie because not one of my relatives can remember his name. They can remember Cousin Puttin taking care of her grandson, but they can't remember his name. He looked like a Chinese with those slanted eyes, cold thick black wavy curly hair with large locks. His skin tone was peachy and flawless with a set of dimples, pure white straight teeth, long legs, long arms, and he too was a talker. He introduced me to the three pure white rabbit, which he kept each in individual cages. They were so pretty and white. We both had to squat down to meet them face-to-face and I enjoyed my first experience feeding those rabbits. It was my father who instructed Charlie to take me outside to feed the rabbits. Charlie's had a vegetable garden three time the size of My Big Mama's and the garden at home, in my backyard. He walked me down each row of this garden, and it was well-managed so like my garden and My Big Mama's garden. He too had to attend to the chicken. They are funny little creatures. When Charlie finished showing me the garden, he extended his long arm for me to take his hand. He walked me up and down the long road near what is now Martin Luther King Jr. Blvd. As soon as my father drove off Estes Pkwy to Old Eldervilled, we turned on either: Bishop St., Beasley St., Morrison St., Craig St., Bronco St., or the new tree named after my relative Johnson St. I understand everything has changed and there are now apartments on that same tree where Cousin Puttin and her grandson lived.

Charlie grabbed my left hand and walked me up and down the street talking forever. His speech was articulate and he was super intelligent. Finally, we came back to the street, and he always instructed me to take a seat near that big huge tree. It was the largest tree I had ever seen in my life. It was a beautiful tree, and I love trees. Charlie never stopped talking but I enjoyed listening to him. When it was time to go, I sat in the back seat behind my father, and I started to cry because I didn't want to leave Charlie. Charlie had tears, in his eyes. Everyone stopped talking and looked at Charlie, then looked at me–we both were crying. From that point, forward, when my father said, "Pack your bags, we are going to the country this weekend, which was nearly every weekend." I adjusted to the raw country life because of Charlie.

My father always stopped in Longview, Texas, before heading home to Dallas. I fed the rabbits, visited Charlie's garden, and walked down the road holding Charlie's hand with his tall self. I remember one time we stopped by to visit, and Charlie was traveling. I was crushed, completely crushed. I did not feed the rabbits, walk down the street, visit the garden, and listen to Charlie talk forever as he held my hand. Years passed by and Charlie was gearing up for college. Right before my father passed away, he shared with me that Charlie was attending a college in New York, studying to become an attorney. I never saw nor heard from Charlie ever again, and his grandmother Cousin Puttin passed away a few years ago. If I had attended the Homegoing Celebration, I may have seen Charlie. One day, perhaps I will travel to Longview, Texas, and pick up Larry and Ruby and have them take me to the funeral homes, located in the area for information and possibly retrieve a copy of the obituary. The family Homecoming Reunion is the first Sunday, in August. I know Cousin Puttin, died a few years after Aunt Myra, which was cousined Puttin's, father's daughter.

Some say, Cousin Puttin was married to a preacher but no one remembers his last name. Charlie held my left hand forever. Likewise, when Robert came to visit me after our first encounter, he reached for my left hand, and he never let go until it was time for me to go inside because the hour was getting late. Robert held a place inside my heart. The longer he held my left hand, the more his spirit increased validating him as my husband. I had never anyone that was able to talk that long and hold my hand atteh same time. His spirit and my spirit united. Likewise, Charlie protected my world, and I could feel his covering of protection. Robert, reminded me of the sincere protection I felt from my cousin from Longview, Texas. I must admit that Robert was not the second person to hold my left hand. Don Williams [Italian mixed with African American], from Tyler, Texas, was the first man who held my hand, while driving walking, walking, attending theatrical performances, and fishing. If we were standing in line at a restaurant waiting to be seated, Don kept my right or left hand locked inside his hand.

Driving to dog training, in Plano, Texas, Jubilee Theatre, in Fort Worth, Texas, Theater Three [inside the Quadrangle], movies, State Fair of Texas, other theatrical events, and places Don held my hand all the way to the location, but he was not the sacred gentleman appointed to envelope my life. While fine dining he fed me like a baby, people watched us instead of eating their own meal. He did all those fine things but he was not the one for me. I remember Don to be a fine gentleman standing 6 feet 2, with dreamy eyes to frame. Women would melt the moment they looked at him. He was very charming and magnetically handsome but with his share of luggage of unnecessary drama. He was open and honest about some of his secrets, but he yet held secrets. Active secrets are unhealthy for any relationship. I met him in the middle 1980's, way before I met Robert, in September 1995.

The first time Robert held my left hand for a number of long hours-never letting go. While he was holding my hand, he was forever sealing my heart completely. That moment meant so much to me, and if I never touch his warm hands again, the memories will last me a lifetime. Locked in my treasured the memories of our first day at the park talking and holding hands. I don't know if he was aware of the registration and stamping of approval my heart was granting to him. Surely, a transfusion of his love was flowing continuously into my spirit causing me to love him deeper. It's rare to meet a gentleman with touching spiritual qualities. Robert knew how to respond, and handle me, which he was a natural flowing into me. He never missed a beat, step, word, or timing. His reactions to me were like a ticking clock with three hands. Every minute, second, and hour was captured, and he arrested each measurement of time tending to me.

Everything Robert said, did, or gestured, validated God's audible spoken words. Only God can provide such a gentleman as such an appointed time. Lately, while driving and thinking retrospectively how protected and guarded my life may have been these last 15 years. He left me unprotected as he answered the call of duty with others guarding and protecting America. Thankful to Robert, and all the military personnel for their major sacrifices keeping us safe. I wonder if Robert knew and know how much spiritual data, which he sealed into my life during our brief two and a half months, which felt like a life time. On April 9, 2011, while driving home from running an errand I thought of Robert, and I laughed remembering his laughter as he was talking about his estate, saying, "Girl, you better ask somebody." I nearly lost control of my vehicle. I lost control of my vehicle momentarily.

Thinking of Robert, I was reminded of the dream, of "THE LION OF JUDAH" with the nucleus nucleolus which the small 'o" appeared inside the letter "O" of the word, "LION." I laughed again at my private thoughts and nearly lost control of the vehicle again. When revelation of a dream comes to you at the most imopertune moment, it's easy to laugh inside and momentarily escape reality, well itappened to me. Robert through God imparted a strong foundation of love for me to stand on remembering his caring love. He released so much of the essence of himself and love into my spiritual data. My heart connected to his heart, and I felt him with me in spite of assuming he was dead. True love lives on regardless of the space of time and the absence of the one you love. True love is timeless and everlasting. True love comes from the soul of your being, and lust is a flesh love, which comes and goes. Lustful love is not stable; it will cause a spouse or partner to seek another one of the flesh while being married to you.

Flesh is not able to hold a person to you. Flesh cannot enter the kingdom of God. The Holy Spirit, which is the Spirit of God dwelling inside of us, will enter heaven. God knows his people because His Spirit dwells inside of them. When this life is over, the spirit of departed soul is absent from the body but present with the LORD about the condition of his heart, which made a permanent deposit, in my memory bank. Robert is a sincere, dedicated, loyal, and committed gentleman. I have learned to execute these two Biblical Scriptures:

(As it is written, I have made thee a father of many nations,) before him whom he believed, even God, who quickeneth the dead, and calleth those things which be not as though they were. Who against hope believed in hope, that he might become the father of many nations, according to that which was spoken, So shall thy seed be. Romans 4:17-18 [KJV]

God reminded me of His spoken words concerning Robert on January 16, 2011. I always thought and wondered about Robert, but actually I thought he was shot down in Bosnia. God was protecting his spoken word that it may prosper at the appointed time. As much as I would love to request the City of Dallas, to shut down the freeway for the dream wedding exchanging wedding vows, in the place where Robert and I first met, the expense and approval might prove to be ridiculously high. Taking a picture at the location for the wedding program, book, and etc. will suffice, but the thought is tempting and it lingers. place to share our story, of how we met.

THE VOICE OF GOD

At the moment, Robert was deployed. I missed him calling and talking with me and surprising me saying, "I am in town." I missed seeing him walk into my mother's front door. She really liked Robert. Probably, because he was tall, handsome, and shared the same first name as her brother, My Uncle Robert Choice, which was murdered near his place of business. People loved my Uncle Robert. I called him Uncle Jr. If anyone bothered me, I called my Uncle Jr, and in no time flat he showed up. He cooked a mean and delicious meat loaf. We often visited him on Sunday's after Worship Service. He owned a restaurant and he knew how to prepare dinner almost better than My Big Mama. I am certain that she taught My Uncle Jr., how to cook with perfection. My uncle lived far away from me, but if I called him, it did not matter. I knew when I saw his truck everything was alright. My father had died and I felt my protection was gone but My Uncle Jr. stepped up to the plate. God sent me one named Robert, which reminds me so much of My Uncle Jr. My Uncle Jr. was a tall and handsome man, and My Aunt Clarkie V. loved her husband.

Likewise, when I wrote my first paragraph at age seven on the front of my grannies white frame home with a black crayon, it was my Uncle Jr, that had to paint the entire house to cover up my paragraph. Watching him paint the house, he would look at me as I was swinging in my swing set. He smiled and laughed to himself. Today, I think I finally understand why he was smiling and laughing, while he was painting and watching me swinging on my swing set near the front gate. My Uncle Jr. was skillful with everything he set out to do. Noticing he moved his latter all around the home until he was finished. I am certain he and My Aunt Clarkie laughed at me a many days about the writing on the front exterior of my grannies' homel. Afterwards, they all gave me so much paper and warned me never to write on the house again. Today, I can laugh about that experience. It's no telling how many people were laughing behind my back, but today, I can laugh. If I could do it all over again, I would write that paragraph for the second time. He was probably thinking. My little niece is going to someday become a writer.

Most children and people write on paper, but my writing on the front of my grannies white frame house was an indication; I desired for people to read my writing. All the cars passed and would notice the writing, and thinking back in retrospect, they may have said, "I know Ms. Fannie nearly had a fit when that child wrote on the front of their home, what nerves." No, it was the beginning of a passion being exercised. It never occurred to me to write my paragraph on a sheet of paper. I wrote on a type of wall for the world to see and read. I wrote on paper in the classroom. It was time to share what I had learned, and I desired for the world to know. Little Mama turned so many different shades of red when she came home and noticed the front of her home.

She was fair complexioned and I had never seen her so mad until she was speechless. I was waiting on a compliment, but she was turning different shades. The first dream I had of Robert after he left for Bosnia, he appeared in my bedroom at my mother's home. The dream was too real, which was near the end of December around Christmas. I assumed that Robert was thinking about me. I started to dream so many dreams of Robert but they are too many to mention. Mentioning only a few is my desire, The next event was a day vision. I had just come in from attending worship service at the Potter's House July 1996. I was tired so sitting on the edge of the bed facing the west, closing my eyes; I saw a cruise ship sailing southward.

Standing in the Lincoln Memorial Cemetery, in a dream October 1998 at midnight watching an African American male digging a grave [I would never visit a graveyard at midnight, so I knew the midnight was significant, but I did not have a clue]. I was facing the north, and he was facing the south. Completing his digging, he pitched the shovel in the dirt with his left hand. Holding the top handle of the shovel, he looked at me, asking, "Linda, do you need a ride home?" "Yes," I replied. Suddenly, I was in three dimensions, seated on a bench inside a private gated estate, standing outside the gate watching a four-door black luxury vehicle drive onto the cobblestone courtyard, and I was standing to the left side of the estate near the garage.

Seeing activity from each direction I focused in on the man driving the black vehicle parking alongside of the garage, which he was facing the front of the estate. Opening the door he stepped out and his legs were long as well as his arms. He walked to the back of his vehicle leaning on the trunk crossing his arms and legs looking at me standing in the entry way to the property. His hair was white, and he wore glasses, but he was young. His disposition was distinctive, distinguished, debonair, authoritatively in-charge, brilliant, and powerful with impeccable taste being one of the high caliber. We looked at each other in silence until the gated was securely closed and locked. I saw myself walking towards his direction. He walked to the front passenger side of the vehicle looking at me seated on the bench. He leaned up against his vehicle and crossed his arms and legs again starring at me.

Seemingly, I was now in two dimensions to the left and seated on the bench. He stood up straight after watching me, saying, "Linda, why are you sitting over there?" I answered him, saying, "Just overlooking the flower garden." He opened his arms wide beckoning for me to stand up and walk to him. I smiled at the gentle standing up walking up to him resting on my head in his chest. We embraced each other mutually for a moment, and we then turned to walk towards the front of the estate hugged up side-to-side. I woke up and called Mother Jenkins [passed away July 22, 2005] on the telephone. She was a seventy-six year old Evangelist, whom I met on September 9, 1995. I was instructed to deliver her a prayer card, which was from the Homegoing Services of her late husband, and he was the senior pastor of their church. She cried the moment. I introduced myself and showed her the prayer card. She broke down crying. She asked me to come inside and take a seat with tears continuously rolling down her cheeks she reached for her bible and started reading scriptures to me. There was no way, I could find a way to tell her. I had to leave because my friend Janet's wedding was starting in about three hours, and I needed to head home to change.

When I looked at her at first glance, she reminded me of my grandmother, My Big Mama. She told me that her daughter Rosie needed to purchase some burial property. The reason for delivering the prayer card was to see if the family required any additional services. I sat with Mother Jenkins for eight hours until her daughter arrived. Mother Jenkins shared the bible with me until her daughter stepped into the door. In those long hours, I learned torightly divide the word of God correctly. I missed Janet's wedding at the hotel, and I knew she would be upset wondering where I was, but I made my first property sale.

Mother Jenkins's daughter purchased burial property. I adopted Mother Jenkins as family. She enjoyed cooking greens, candy yams, and lots of vegetables. My financial budget was tight, but I would always stop by Famers Market Downtown Dallas and purchase her several bunch of greens, okra, squash, yams, and bottled water. She drank soda because she did not like to drink water, but she would drink the expensive bottled water. Every time we talked in person or over the telephone she would reach for her bible and share the word of God with me. I met Robert about two weeks later, after meeting Mother Jenkins. I called her to tell her I had met someone while driving on the freeway. Her first words, "Watch out, you are driving a brand new vehicle." I said, "Yes, Ma am." Pondering the experience of the audible words spoken from God, and the fact that Robert was driving a brand new Cadillac. The memory of the mesmerizing moment was refreshing to me, so I decided to ponder the memories.

The first time I heard the small still voice of God. I was seven years old. Seated on the wooden steps of my grannies' home I heard the small still voice speak clearly. I walked inside and stood in the kitchen and suddenly out of nowhere I felt an evil spirit. Perplexed, I pondered the experiences. I knew my grannies would understand because they held a weekly prayer meeting, in their living room each with an additional twelve senior citizen, which were all females with white hair. They prayed warfare payer standing up moving their hands like Indian warriors. It was mentioned that My Big Mama was Cherokee Indian. She always instructed me to take a seat next to her and do not move.

My duties were to greet the ladies with warm hospitality when they arrived at the front door. I offered them either Danish, slice of cake, coffee, or tea. They were always returning my greetings and flooding me with kisses on my cheeks. Feeling their sincere heartfelt love, I smiled and reciprocated their kind appreciations. Never uttering one word of the message, that was spoken to me from the small still voice of God while seated on the back porch steps. Immediately, when I walked back inside standing near the kitchen, I felt something evil. I stopped in my tracks. I was standing in the kitchen near the front bedroom door. Since learning, when God spoke a word, you will face attacks, which is the validation and confirmation it came from God. So keeping certain information within to ponder was easy for me. I was watching My Big Mama, and I knew when to speak, and when not to speak. Knowing Mother Jenkins was being protective I pondered.

She knew about the gentleman I stopped seeing and advised me to stop answering my telephone when he called me, saying, "No answer is a message." She did not care much for his character and never wanted to hear anything else about him because she said he was totally wrong for me, and she never wanted to meet him, the friend or no friend. I understood her reasoning, and he never got a chance to meet Mother Jenkins. I desired for Robert to meet Mother Jenkins, especially after he has sung that gospel song to me outside in the openness of nature. Unequivocally, Mother Jenkins would have fallen in love with Robert and blessed us to marry. He was deployed to Bosnia, so I never got the chance to introduce him to a beautiful woman of God. She came to the fashion show project, which Robert missed because he was traveling. She did not care for the secular portion of the show, but she enjoyed the gospel singing.

Knowing she was particular I took a chance but her daughter Rose was on stage singing. She instructed me to never invite her to a mixture of gospel and secular events combined. Desiring to tell her that Jesus spoke to people that knew nothing about him, but they were converted because he spoke meaning and purpose into their lives, so I again pondered my words. When I woke up from the dream of being in the grave at midnight and having the grave digger, which drove me to a private gated estate-I woke Mother Jenkins up early in the morning. After I shared the dream. to her, she shared something with me.

She said, "Your dream is clear. You do not need me to interpret but the man digging the grave is the one you need to get far away from, and the man at the private gated estate is your husband." I figured that much but on March 31, 2011, as I completed the recording of a live radio broadcast on Blog Talk Radio, the word midnight lit up bright with revelation:

And at midnight Paul and Silas prayed, and sang praises unto God: and the prisoners heard them. And suddenly there was a great earthquake, so that the foundations of the prison were shaken: and immediately all the doors were opened, and every one's bands were loosed. [Acts 16:25-26 KJV]

And it came to pass at midnight , that the man was afraid , and turned himself: and, behold, a woman lay at his feet. [Ruth 3:8]

When midnight passes, the manifestation shall come forth. The midnight produces structure, alignment, and spiritual maturity. A blessing of a major magnitude requires a foundation of discipline. God will prepare you for his glory. The greater the misery, the greater the blessing is often spoken to serve notice to the chosen to look beyond the pain and press your way to the higher calling.

For his anger endureth but a moment; in his favour is life: weeping may endure for a night, but joy cometh in the morning. Psalm 30:5 [KJV]

Midnight is the development to help you manage the blessing. Money, power and status are weapons the devil may use to trip and trick you but when you are grounded in the knowledge. I knew to surround myself with godly people that are rooted and not easily tainted with an abundance of charming words and flattering ways. I knew to become planted like a tree. Association with bad company may damage character if you shift and change while under the influence. King Solomon stood a chance but he started associating with the wrong negative company. Demons transfer, and the greater the crowd, contacts, and circle of people, a strong prayer with fasting is required.

I heard what Mother Jenkins had to say, but I too heard the audible voice of God. It's so easy to cancel God's word and listen to man's word. Most times it's not that you are trying to be disobedient, but you sense you are listening to one seasoned with godly wisdom. As right as it may sound, when you know you heard from God-keep praying to avoid cancelling God's word to obey man. A quick answer or opinion without prayer, may the flesh responding. When I speak of the audible voice of God, I am referring to a message from God [small still voice, angel/messenger, and, etc.].

THE CASE BETWEEN
ELI AND HANNAH

*I*t's so easy for people to misunderstand and assume the wrong messages even when they are anointed, skilled with expertise, and especially great leaders. I like to acknowledge that Eli was a priest. Consequently, the people we know and respect are human and they too make mistakes.

So Hannah rose up after they had eaten in Shiloh, and after they had drunk. Now Eli the priest sat upon a seat by a post of the temple of the LORD. I Samuel 1:9 [KJV]

Hannah experienced a confrontation with Elkanah her husband's other wife Peninnah. You see Peninnah had children by Elkanah, but Hannah had no children. Her womb was shut up [I Samuel 1:2, 3-5 KJV].

And her adversary also provoked her sore, for to make her fret, because the LORD had shut up her womb. [1 Samuel 1:6 KJV]

And she vowed a vow and said, O LORD of hosts, if thou wilt indeed look on the affliction of thine handmaid, and remember me, and not forget thine handmaid, but wilt give unto thine handmaid a man child, then I will give him unto the LORD all the days of his life, and there shall no razor come upon his head. [I Samuel 1:11 KJV]

Listen to the words Hannah expressed to Eli:

And it came to pass, as she continued praying before the LORD, that Eli marked her mouth. 1 Samuel 1:12

And Hannah answered and said, No, my lord, I am a woman of a sorrowful spirit: I have drunk neither wine nor strong drink, but have poured out my soul before the LORD. I Samuel 1:15[KJV]

Eli the priest stood corrected:

Then Eli answered and said, Go in peace: and the God of Israel grant thee thy petition that thou hast asked of him. 1 Samuel 1:17 [KJV]

An incident happened with her son Samuel when God was calling Samuel when Eli was old but Samuel was wise. [1 Samuel 2:22].

And it came to pass at that time, when Eli was laid down in his place, and his eyes began to wax dim, that he could not see; And were the lamp of God went out in the temple of the LORD, where the ark of God was, and Samuel was laid down to sleep; That the LORD called Samuel: and he answered, Here am I. 1 Samuel 3:2-4 [KJV]

The LORD was calling Samuel, but Samuel thought it was the voice of Eli.

And the LORD called Samuel again the third time. And he arose and went to Eli, and said, Here am I; for thou didst call me. And Eli perceived that the LORD had called the child. 1 Samuel 3:8 [KJV]

Therefore Eli said unto Samuel, Go, lie down: and it shall be, if the call thee, that thou shalt say, Speak, LORD; for thy servant heareth. So Samuel went and lay down in his place. And the LORD came, and stood, and called as at other times, Samuel, Samuel. Then Samuel answered, Speak; for thy servant heareth. And the LORD said to Samuel, Behold, I will do a thing in Israel, at which both the ears of every one that heareth it shall tingle. 1 Samuel 9-11[KJV]

In that day I will perform against Eli all things which I have spoken concerning his house: when I begin, I will also make an end. [1 Samuel 9:12 [KJV]

When God speaks, we are to listen and value his spoken word. I respected Mother Jenkins and I knew to simply listen and not a reason with her. The dream of being in the grave at midnight meant I would experience a midnight journey before the manifestation of the fruition. As like, Joseph, the son of Israel/Jacob. No one knows how long a spiritual midnight will last before the joy came in the morning. The dream started out at midnight, but when I arrived at the private gated estate it was daylight and the man was driving into the gate.

THE DREAM OF THE
JET EXPLODING

*A*nother major dream I did not understand was with the jet, which exploded in midair directly over my backyard, in a dream on February 13, 2006. The dream started with me standing in my backyard holding a thick rope or oversized lasso. One end was in my right hand, and the other end was around the front of the jet. The jet flew at high altitude flying north. The rope was intact and attached during the entire dream. Suddenly, the jet reached high altitude standing at a thick white framed window in the northern sky eastward. He waited was long but I stood patiently holding the other end of the rope, which was around the front of the jet.

It felt as if I had been waiting for hours. Finally, the jet was granted permission to enter. Seeing the rope around the front of the jet, and the other end securely in my right hand. I could see around the throne. The jet was standing in midair directly in front of the throne. Hearing the voice of authority speaking but I was not able to understand the words. This wait was longer than the first wait but again, I stood there patiently holding the rope trying to figure why the rope was in my hand and attached around the front of the jet.

Finally, the jet was leaving the throne and the rope secure around the front of the jet and held in my right hand. Half way from the throne the jet looked as if it was experiencing severe turbulence flying southward near the east. Quickly, the jet was flying directly over my backyard with the rope remaining the same. I could hear the sound of the jet for it was not positioned in midair over my backyard near even with the top of my roof. Once the jet was directly over my backyard, it exploded in midair. The right wing fell down to the ground, and the rope was around the right wing as it hit the ground.

I heard a voice say, release the rope. I slowly bent down as I laid the rope on the ground, and I turned walking to the front of this home noticing I was suddenly in a brand new neighborhood but the explosion caused a home to catch fire. I ran inside to see the back of a sofa on fire. There inside was a male friend name Paul, which he is a preacher's kid, and his father was a superintended whom recently passed away [2011]. I grabbed Paul to guide him out of the home without causing him to panic.

Paul had only a few burned spots on his back, but he was disoriented so I put the fire out on his back and I put the fire out that was burning on the back of his sofa. He was not able to comprehend what was happening. So I took him slowly by the hand guiding him outside. He slowly took my lead, but he appeared detached from life. Walking him slowly down the sidewalk I noticed my home turned into an estate. I do not live in an estate. When I came to my home, in the dream, it had seven steps leading up the double doors. It was actually a beautiful estate.

I considered them the model family of the neighborhood besides My Big Mama's home environment. Everything appeared to be perfect in their home and Paul's parents were strict with balance. They were seemingly always happy, and I enjoyed playing ball with them in their backyard, which My Big Mama could always stand on the her front porch and see me outside playing. They are yet the most adorable and honest people I know. It was three sons and two daughters, again, which I adopted as my brothers and sisters. They are genuine people with pure hearts and clean hands.

Attending church service with them many times was always pleasurable. I adopted them as my second family. Admiring their mother, which Sister Fields was so graceful, poised soft spoken, and classy. Peace was what I felt being around their family, and it felt the same as being in the midst of my grannies and those twelve senior citizens that prayed each week.

The moment I stood in the midst of a person with evil intent, I felt my peace leave me, which I had a point-of-reference from age seven. I am able to identify when the worker of an enemy is employed by the Prince of the Air, you can feel the spirit. I knew to stay far away from those people because they were not to be trusted. Even so, as I grew, I had to attend school, work, and relate to people that were not born again believers, but I knew nothing about pleading the blood of Jesus. Lacking knowledge of the Holy Ghost. I knew how to pray, and I knew when my peace left and what an evil spirit felt like but my knowledge was limited. I had to be social but God knows I required some spiritual education.

THE ACCOUNTANT

My dear friend Glenn, the accountant. Repeatedly, Glenn kept asking me to fly to Houston, Texas to meet his family, and he was so excited and adamant until I had to tell him, "I will not be flying to Houston, Texas ever, and never." He insisted on knowing the reason, why so I shared with him the truth. Every Friday evening, he would pick me up and drive me all the way to DFW to watch the airplanes' land and take off while dining at the airport. That made it worse. He tried that scene for two whole months, and he finally gave up and drove me to Fort Worth, Texas. When I walked into the door his entire family flew here to meet me. His beautiful sister is a flight attendant. His grandmother she too was very beautiful even in her golden years, which the entire family was mixed with Creo, French, Italian, and other. When I stepped into the front door, I was sweetly surprised to see his entire family had flown in order to meet me.

His grandmother extended both her arms out beckoning for me to come and take a seat on the sofa next to her. She held my hand during the entire visit. His family was king and with warm hospitable spirits. His mom was a gorgeous lady and his father handsome. His grandmother's hair was silver white and very long hanging all the way down her back. We laughed the night away and the evening was most enjoyable. My Little Mama was upset because Glenn was seven years older than me, and he was sending me back to college and paying for my entire education. She saw me ironing his shirts and started asking questions about him after I met his family. She insisted that I date someone closer to my own age, so I had to break off the relationship, which was a terrible mistake listening to my granny this time.

While working at the corporate office of a business on the west end of Stemmons Freeway, in accounting. I saw Glenn in a wedding photo as a best man. My heart skipped a beat, and the owner did not know how to remain in touch with him. A few years later, I went out to Bernard's with a friend. She asked me to come alone, there was Glenn seated with his colleague from work. He ran up to me taking a seat at the bar telling me how his grandmother gave me her favorite scarf and how he would park down the street from my mother's hoping and waiting for me to come outside the gate, so he could ask me to marry him but that day never came. He didn't know if I had married someone or not so he dared not move to swiftly by walking up to the front door. He said, "I parked down the street for two straight weeks every evening." I knew Glenn loved me because if I sneezed, he sent me a get well card in the mail, and he loved to eat tomato soup. He often shared with me his fraternity days and all the things he had to do to pledge. When I met Glenn, I was on my way to the ladies' room with all my girlfriends, we dared not separate-we stayed together. If we danced, we all stood on the dance floor together. Glenn was seated far away from the crowd of people, and he was too preppy to be an ordinary guy.

I was in a tight, so I was walking fast. When I came close to pass his table, he reached out and grabbed my left hand. I looked at him knowing he was of a higher caliber from every gentleman in the room. He was the handsome studio and he wore glasses. He was six feet two inches tall, slender and well-groomed. His skin was extremely fair complexioned. You could tell he was a business man. I gestured to him that I was in a tight, and I would be right back. I told the girls that I was going to stop and speak to the gentleman who grabbed my hand. He too was a talker and had so many positive essential contents to share in his conversation. He did not have any negative things to share, but he spoke extensively about education and higher learning. He was brilliant with the application of accounting. When he shared with me about the chicken, we laughed so hard together, and I shared with Glenn how I tended to the chicken in my grannies' backyard and how the roosters would chase me all over the backyard after gathering the eggs from the chicken coup. I know how funny the chicken could I but his time of sharing was funnier, and he kept me laughing. He shared more stories of his college life each Friday on the way to DFW Airport. Glenn tried so hard to get me on the airplane. I may have established the phobic from being physically and mentally abused from age eight to sixteen.

04/21/2011 Partially, I survived through journaling but God carried me through it all. God was with me even when I had no idea God had angels around me protecting from day to day. I enjoyed listening to Glenn share his college experiences, and he knew I too desired to return so he offered to pay for my full education. His family was wealthy but Glenn was very conservative. He would mention the word budget and personal budget in every conversation and all I thought about was shopping. Asking myself, "How will I ever get a chance to go shopping being married to a conservative man?" every day we spoke. His grandmother passed away. He married someone else and they had a son together. I ran into Glenn a few years later but things had changed. I moved losing contact with him. Glenn shared with me that his grandmother told him to be sure and marry me. We laughed and I gave him my new number and My Little Mama had passed listening to her caused me to make the wrong decision. I believe to this day. Glenn's grandmother instructed him to have my iron his shirts, and if I did–I would make a good wife.

Glenn's shirts were always heavenly starched as so when I first met him, which meant he made frequent the cleaners for that quality starch. I too prepared my cotton shirts with extra heavy starch for the fresh crisp look. I wore the designer baggy pants with the high heel pumps, and heavily starched cotton blouses and shirt like My Big Mama.

My shoes had to be sharp and expensive and black, brown, or navy blue. Having the taste of a conservative tailored fashion style may have captured Glenn's attention. My favorite color was the deep navy blue. The conservative black was nice but the navy blue reminded me of the sky at night. The white was my reminder of the beautiful white thick clouds I would watch waiting for God to show me his face as a small child. Glenn may have made me the perfect husband because he was domineering and confident. I missed the opportunity of being married to the most wonderful husband. Perhaps marrying Glenn was not in the provision.

His mom was a gorgeous lady and his father handsome. His grandmother's hair was silver white and very long hanging all the way down her back. We laughed the night away and the evening was most enjoyable. My Little Mama was upset because Glenn was seven years older than me, and he was sending me back to college and paying for my entire education. She saw me ironing his shirts and started asking questions about him after I met his family. She insisted that I date someone closer to my own age, so I had to break off the relationship, which was a terrible mistake listening to my granny this time.

While working at the corporate office of a business on the west end of Stemmons Freeway, in accounting. I saw Glenn in a wedding photo as a best man. My heart skipped a beat, and the owner did not know how to locate Glenn. A few years later, I went out to Bernard's with a friend. She asked me to come alone at the last minute. When I arrived, I walked straight into Glenn seated with his colleague from work. He ran up to me taking a seat at the bar sharing with me how his grandmother instructed him to marry me, and how he would park down the street from my mother's hoping and waiting for me to come outside the gate, so he could ask me to marry him but that day never came. He didn't know if I had married someone or not so he dared not move to swiftly by walking up to the front door. He said, "I parked down the street for two straight weeks every evening." I knew Glenn loved me because if I sneezed he sent me a get well card in the mail, and he loved to eat tomato soup. He often shared with me his fraternity days and all the things he had to do to pledge. When I met Glenn, I was on my way to the ladies' room with all my girlfriends, we dared not separate-we stayed together. If we danced, we all stood on the dance floor together. Glenn was seated far away from the crowd of people, and he was too preppy to be an ordinary guy.

I was in a tight, so I was walking fast. When I came close to pass his table, he reached out and grabbed my left hand. I looked at him knowing he was of a higher caliber from every gentleman in the room. He was the handsome studio and he wore glasses. He was six feet two inches tall, slender and well-groomed. His skin was extremely fair complexioned. You could tell he was a business man. I gestured to him that I was in a tight, and I would be right back. I told the girls that I was going to stop and speak to the gentleman who grabbed my hand. He too was a talker and had so many positive essential contents to share in his conversation. He did not have any negative things to share, but he spoke extensively about education and higher learning. He was brilliant with the application of accounting. When he shared with me the details concerning the chicken he had to kiss for initiation, which was part of the initiation process to become gain membership to gain membership into a particular fraternity. Glenn, and I share many moments of laughter, about college, airplanes, accounting, and I have heard that laughter is medicine for the internal body. We shared so many laughs about his college it made me want to experience a four year college, but I desired to learn English to be an excellent writer and to teach children early to write with excellence.

It was so much fun hanging out with Glenn because he was highly educated and he talked a lot about education. His college experience was exciting to me, which I was all ears. And I shared with Glenn how I tended to the chicken in my grannies' backyard and how the roosters would chase me all over the backyard after gathering the eggs from the chicken coup. I know how funny the chicken could me but his time of sharing was funnier, and he kept me laughing. He shared more stories of his college life each Friday on the way to DFW Airport. Glenn tried so hard to get me on the airplane. I may have established the phobic from being physically and mentally abused from age eight to sixteen.

Partially, I survived through journaling but God carried me through it all. God was with me even when I had no idea God had angels around me protecting from day to day. I enjoyed listening to Glenn share his college experiences, and he knew I too desired to return so he offered to pay for my full education. His family was wealthy but Glenn was very conservative. He would mention the word budget and personal budget in every conversation and all I thought about was shopping. Asking myself, "How will I ever get a chance to go shopping being married to a conservative man?" every day we spoke. His grandmother passed away. He married someone else and they had a son together. I ran into Glenn a few years later but things had changed. I moved losing contact with him. Glenn shared with me that his grandmother told him to be sure and marry me. We laughed and I gave him my new number and My Little Mama had passed listening to her caused me to make the wrong decision. I believe to this day. Glenn's grandmother instructed him to have my iron his shirts, and if I did–I would make a good wife.

Glenn's shirts were always heavenly starched as so when I first met him, which meant he made frequent the cleaners for that quality starch. I too prepared my cotton shirts with extra heavy starch for the fresh crisp look. I wore the designer baggy pants with the high heel pumps, and heavily starched cotton blouses and shirt like My Big Mama. She always looked so crispy and refreshed, in her healthy vibrant days.

My shoes had to be sharp and expensive and black, brown, or navy blue. Having the taste of a conservative tailored fashion style may have captured Glenn's attention. My favorite color is the deep navy blue.

The conservative black was nice but the navy blue reminded me of the sky at night. The white was my reminder of the beautiful white thick clouds, which I would watch waiting for God to show me his face as a small child. Glenn may have made me the perfect husband because he was domineering, authoritative, and confident. I adored his family, and they would have been the perfect in laws. His grandmother stole my heart.

Her spirit and demeanor reminded me of My Big Mama. I missed the opportunity of being married to the most wonderful husband. I guess, it was not meant to be. Glenn always talked about his family and after meeting them, I understood why. It was the perfect family for me. They would not have had to wait to invite me to come and visit them in Houston, Texas. I would have caught a flight with Glenn to surprise them spontaneously. I enjoy being around good people. His grandmother, would have acquired a loyal friend, I would have done everything in the world for her. When I think of the acceptance and love, I felt from his family and from Glenn why God allowed me to miss the blessing of being married into a wonderful family. They were beautiful people inside and out. His name is Glenn Fisher. He was the epitome of a gentleman. Glenn was the best missed opportunity and would have made the perfect husband. I sense they were mixed with CEO and lots of French.

MEETING MINISTER RON

*T*oday, while in class, I realized how much I miss Robert. I shared with God how much I miss him. It's amazing how protected and secure I felt in the short time. I meet him before he was deployed. I lived on the telephone with him. Enjoying his conversation, and remembering the walk, he walked to my vehicle. Thinking of the soothing sound of his singing voice, and the hours he held my hand sharing his deep secrets. To be honest, the last time I truly felt that secure was when I was a tiny little girl spending time with My Big Mama. She was the mirror of epitome illustrating authentic love, and I felt the same the first time I met Robert on Stemmons Freeway heading southbound. I had never seen a strong authoritative man share his vulnerability in private.

He shared the breaking of his heart. with me. It was shared between the two of us, which were appointed to respect each other without hesitation. I met a minister from Fort Worth, Texas name Ron F. He was about 6 feet 3 or 4. I had a taste for some cranberry juice to add a few fresh orange slices for a really soothing healthy and tasty drink. The sliced oranges enhance the flavor. With my love for magazine, I should say, expensive magazine. I ran a quick errand to Winn Dixie before they closed the store location on Westmoreland. Craving some cranberry juice, which I just had to have. I enjoy the taste of cranberry juice with orange slices. Whenever I visit the grocery store, I often take about an hour retreat near the magazine rack to review expensive magazines.

My favorite magazine is Florida Design. I discovered the magazine one day after having the dream of being in the graveyard at Lincoln Memorial Cemetery at midnight, in October 1998. The second part of the dream detailed a private gated estate with a cobblestone courtyard, my husband, and a black four-door vehicle. He is tall, with white hair, and he wears glasses. His legs and arms are long. His physic is slender and athletically toned. He is a gentleman of great distinction and caliber. He can throw his weight around.

Well, after having the dream, which I believe was the third day, I went to the Albertson's grocery store on West Davis and Hampton road, which was a newly constructed store. I enjoyed the fresh crispy atmosphere, but I loved the magazine rack. It was always neatly supplied with expensive magazines. The kind, I enjoyed with the very expensive estate and fine décor. In fact, the best time was when the new magazines were fleshly stocked on the shelves. Taking notice to the cover of the Florida Design magazine-I opened the magazine thinking I was going to glance through the page and enjoy my private retreat. The managers never approached me probably because I spent so much on groceries each week. I knew to keep the pages neat for purchase. I started flipping through the pages and much to my surprise the same exact estate was being showcased in the magazine. It shocked me so bad until I screamed so loud.

Everyone in the store within my view froze. They probably thought I was being robbed. I quickly started flipping the pages, so they would continue their business. Especially if the new magazine issues were out on the stand I would stand and glance through the pages. I had been standing there for nearly thirty minutes, and I noticed this tall flawless gentleman walk into the store. I never turned to look, but I could see him from my peripheral vision. His energy was high and he was extremely confident. I never turned to his directions. Finally, I went down the aisle to grab my cranberry juice to head home. While checking for sugar contents, I noticed he was still in the store, but I never turned to his attention.

Seeing him walk backwards, I knew he was coming down the aisle. He said, "You are holding on to that cart, and all you have is a bottle of cranberry juice." Before I could say something smart, he said, "Don't know the woman allow me to pass by her without her speaking to me." I dropped the bottle into the cart and turned to look at him straight into his face. He was very handsome, that kind of flawless handsome, and he knew it. I said, "You are handsome, but you are not all that. OK." He looked surprise that I addressed him without fear or flirtation. Standing and giving him a blank look, waiting for him to say something else stupid. "Where do you attend church?" He asked. When I answered him, he said, "That figures, I should have known." I was a member of a mega church under the leadership of a mega minister.

My church membership had nothing to do with my response to him. He was arrogant, conceited, and self-centered beyond tolerance, and he knew he was a prime pick for desperate women. He said, "I do not understand, why you did not come on to me." I looked at him wanting to know if he was really serious or was he pulling my leg with a unique hello. He was serious. I switch to my on private news channel to broadcast him developing "Breaking News." I had to snap my right finger up in the air to announce the urgency of the news-you are very handsome, but you are not all of that-OK. He stood there looking at me speechless for about five minutes. There was complete silence. I was hoping he got the message. He looked as if he completely tuned into the news because he was in the spotlight of my news mental news camera. It was pointed directly on him. The next words that came out of his mouth was the question, "Where do you attend church? Let me guess, the Potter's House, because you ladies are some the smartest talking women I have ever met."

Standing there looking into his eyes he waited for me to say something smart, but I lowered my voice to a soft gentle tone, saying, "Yes, I am a member of the Potter's House but that have nothing to do with the words I spoke." Sharing with him how detestable and offensive his words. We stood in the aisle talking for three hours and finally. I expressed to him. I needed to go home. He asked, "I like to talk to you, will you call me?" I agreed, and he gave me his business card. When I learned that he was a minister and astute in bible study. I had words for him. He was a ready preaching machine, and his senior pastor was preparing to send him to the nations.

At the time he had a twelve year old daughter, and he drove a brand new black Range Rover, which was a gift from a professional basketball player. He invited me to attend his ordination and sit on the front row because those single women were lying on him at church because he refuses to date them. I considered attending until he said what he said, trying to make me a target. Fort Worth being too far to drive to come outside to my vehicle destroyed. I know silly women, and I refuse to be designated as a prime target. He talked over the telephone, and Ron would preach sermons to me over the telephone. One evening he drove all the way to Dallas.

to Dallas, Texas to talk to me face-to-face. I came outside and we talked, while seated in his black on black Range Rover. We were having a decent conversation until he said, "If I married you, you will obey me. What ever I tell you to do-you will do it." His tone was authoritative and we were not dating." I asked him to unlock the door for a minute. I jumped out his vehicle and went inside. He kept calling the home telephone apologizing, saying, he was just kidding. I told him to go home. A desperate woman would have accepted his out of place tone. I felt he was testing me and I was not in the mood.

The last conversation I had with Ron, he said that I was different, and it was refreshing. He said, he met so many beautiful women, but they were shallow and there was no interest. Ron was searching for substance, but he was in much need to surrender his all before God to understand his position as a minister. I pray he is being a blessing to the Kingdom Building Business of God. God will use him mightily. He too owned several Mercedes Benz and three detailed shops. Ron loves to study the bible deeply. He was not perfect and neither am I. He too is a powerful man of God, and would make a great husband. Ron and I could talk extensively about scripture and life. We would live on the telephone for hours reading and talking about scripture. One day, I hope to see Ron again.

SEPTEMBER 1, 1996

*T*he day of September 1, 1996, presented a significant experience, while seated in the sanctuary of a mega church. I was seated with the young lady, that invited me to visit the church, and it was about my fourth visit to this church. Waking up early to prepare for church. I heard the small still voice of God, saying, "Join the church today." Being no stranger to hearing his voice, I kept those words to myself, and I was in agreement to join during the altar call. My heart was heavy with the weight of concerns. The person that invited me to attend picked me up to making sure I would attend.

With her. I was a current member of another mega church located in the same cities. We were early, and the church was mostly empty except for about a hundred and fifty people scattered all over the church engaged in group conversations. The person that invited me was talking to her friends on my left. So I sat there waiting silently and alone not talking for church to start. Thinking of the hurtful things in life tears were trying to visit and comfort me, but I begged them not to appear. , Suddenly, walking down my empty pew was a gentleman named Ricco; he was in the company of another tall gentleman with bright red hair.

Looking at him reminded me of the late Lucille Ball. They both spoke and took a seat right next to me on my right. Noticing they were extremely tall and slender, well-groomed, and distinctive. Ricco was sharing information with the other gentleman about the leader and the church. Then he turned to me, and asked my name and a long conversation manifested between the two of us. He relaxed his left arm over the back of my pew and probably seeing the tears I tried so hard to control. he took my left hand with his right hand and continuing, talking to me and asking me how long had I been saved.

The lady who invited me took noticed of him holding my hand or one of the ladies in the group beckoned her to look. She privately hit me in my side whispering into my ear, asking, "Who is that good-looking man?" Knowing I would not get rid of her until I introduced everyone to each other. They were both fine well-manaered gentlemen. After the introduction, she started eavesdropping in on my conversation finding it difficult to continue talking with her friends. Ricco shared with me that he and he fellow classmate where students from Christ for the Nations. He explained to me how serious their walk with the LORD, prayer service, his major.

Looking down at hand, I noticed a ring on the wedding finger. Raising my head to look into his eyes, knowing the look of one not telling the truth, I asked, "Are you married?" He knew I had caught a glimpse of the band on the wedding finger. He said, "The ring is a celibacy ring, which I vowed celibacy until I am married. Sharing with me the ceremony conducted before the ring was placed on his finger. "I made a promise to only give myself to my wife, when I marry." That was the first time I had ever heard a handsome man speak with such character, dignity, and commitment to honor God. Checking his classmate finger, he too was wearing the same band. My spirit perked up because I was seated next to two gentlemen of spiritual pureness and spiritual quality.

Ricco was born and raised in Puerto Ricco. As worship service was preparing to start, Ricco looked into my eyes, saying, "The Lord, said, 'You are to join this church today,' Today." I looked at him as were releasing our hands, and I said, "I know, the Lord whisper the same to me before I left home." Ricco smiled, and worship service started. The senior pastor and his wife stood together on the pulpit instructing everyone to take hold of persons' hands face each other and repeat after me. Ricco stood before holding both my hands, and he was much taller over me, so I had to look up into his eyes.

Every word the pastor announced Ricco repeated the words exactly to me. Tears came pouring down his cheeks, and I was trying to keep a straight face. I had never seen a handsome man cry like that before in my life. The words were powerful, and Ricco never broke eye contact with me. It was my turn to repeat the word as they were released from the pastor, which was the longest repeat of words. The tears continued to roll down Ricco cheeks and as the final words were repeated Ricco stood there looking down into my eyes; he embraced me with tears in his eyes. My life was healed. Every tear begging to fall from my eyes vanished, and the pain, hurt, and disappointment I carried left me completely.

Standing before him on September 1, 1996, felt as if I were standing on an altar of marriage exchanging vows. Thinking back, I believe God was allowing me to practice the holiness of exchanging wedding vows for a covenant marriage. The experience with Ricco husband immediately covers you under his umbrella, but he must my holy and connected with the LORD spiritually, naturally, and willing to sacrifice his flesh to obey God.

Perhaps, just perhaps, Ricco was standing in the gap preparing me for Robert. Each gentleman I met was preparing me to decrease my feisty nature to a simmer. I had no problem being feisty, but there comes a time when empathy and maturity are ready to rule with discipline. There was so much anger silently living inside until I may have run any potential mate away that crossed me, the wrong way, or I would have walked out on the marriage. Standing before Ricco, I realized that a man is human. He can be gentle, strong, and he might even cry, and return immediately to his strength. A man may suffer hurt just like an emotional woman but his ego, in my opinion, is connected to his masculinity. My feisty defense to protect Linda, may have injured a marriage. Wondering if God allowed Robert to be deployed to prepare me to be a better wife. God knew Robert's desires what Robert desired, in a wife. Likewise, he God knew what kind of gentleman I deserved. We took our seats and Ricco, reached for my hand and held my hand all through morning worship service, and he never let go of my hand until the invitation came to join the church.

He looked into my eyes and said, "Remember. You are to join this church today." I said, "I know." Making my way out the pew to the altar I stood in obedience, but I felt this aura standing directly behind me. Having an inquisitive nature, I turned to look behind me; there stood Ricco standing directly behind me. He too was joining the same church.

JANUARY 16, 2011

After fifteen years of not seeing or hearing from Robert, I have a dream of him. When I came in from church, I was perplexed concerning a matter. Feeling awful I prayed and went to bed early. The first dream was of seeing Robert appear in the detached isolated pure white window. I prayed before I closed my eyes to go to bed. Suddenly, I felt a presence in my room, and it was thick, and I was to take notice by waking up. With my eyes open in a vision, while in a dream. I saw Roberts's face in the window. He was attired in a navy blue sports jacket, designer navy shirt with thin white stripes. In his same authoritative voice he said, "Linda, come out side." I remember closing my eyes turning over to go back to sleep but in the dream I jumped up from my bed running outside to greet him jumping high upon his waist saying, "It so good to see you." I jumped down yet dancing and saying, "I am so glad to see you." The look on his face was phlegmatic, and he looked at me with a serious look waiting for me to stop dancing. I stopped. He stood direct looking into my eyes to make certain I was paying attention. He raised his left hand pointing to the south, saying, "I DID THIS FOR YOU." Suddenly, a beautiful estate appeared right before my eyes. I cared nothing about the estate because I was so glad to see Robert after all these years. I jumped back up on his waist, and he was finally cheerful. I hugged him, again, saying, "I am so glad to see you. He smiled, saying, "Let me see your foot." I kicked my right let up in the air and pulled off the black sock exposing my toes, which were painted with bright red toe nail polish. I wiggled my toes and we both started laughing. I woke up out of the dream. Then I jumped up out of the bed running to the back door . I looked outside and there was no one standing there. But the spot where he stood in the dream was the same spot where the jet exploded and the right wing fell down from the sky with the lasso/rope from the dream I dreamed on February 13, 2006. Wearing black house sock with the rubber under the bottom I greeted Robert with exuberance. The second dream placed me downtown Dallas riding the bus into Downtown Dallas. When I stepped off the bus, I stepped onto the mail truck. Another lady boarded with me. Then this rather large lady wearing a baby blue two piece suit tried to board and the truck, and the truck nearly fell over. I said to her we need to balance the weight. She was trying to sit right next to me. Finally, I moved to the back and the heavy lady in the blue suit drove the mail truck. When we reached the other side of downtown Dallas, she mentioned they allow her to use the truck to attend her church events.

I then asked her to give me a call, so I can attend the next event. She gave me two business cards. I passed one to the lady on my right. She flipped my business card over saying, "You don't have much money" I asked her, "Why" and she said, "You printed your business cards on old paper, and the checking account number is on the back. I looked at the numbers, and they appeared to be bank transaction codes. I then asked the driver wearing the baby blue suit to drive me to the other side of downtown. I managed to arrive at the Key Hole building. I then woke. I understand the meaning of the Key Hole building from the dream on December 20, 2001. I was in a large conservative conference room on the 28th floor with a team of financial attorney organizing my financial portfolio. Looking out the window I saw something amazing outside the glass window facing the southeast. The double dream switched over to the top of the bank plaza with a team of trust officers completing my financial profile. Once the details of the financial package were sealed. I returned to the key hole building the attorney's. I woke up thinking wow! The key hole building is my favorite building in Downtown Dallas. Every time I drive to Sunflower Market. I make sure I drive down Ross Ave to behold the beauty of the amazing architects.

The next dream started as I was in my bedroom room, and **Robert** appeared in an isolated window calling out my name **asking me** to come outside in the backyard.

A MILITARY SOLDIER

There is so much to learn about Robert and his first beginning in the military. Hopefully, and prayerfully, I am looking forward to greeting Robert personally once again. First, I will thank him for serving our country as a military solider. Secondly, I will thank him for protecting me from a distance serving in the capacity as a military aviation combat pilot. While waiting to see Robert again, I felt compelled to watch romantic movies about military soldiers, and I enjoy each movie. I own a classic military movie titled, *"Anne of Green Gables."* There is something amazing about this movie, and I can relate to her very well. I had to own my copies to watch and remember Robert as often as I desired. It's a beautiful collection. I found the movies watching the advertisement on television after I met Robert and after his deployment to Bosnia. I enjoy reading about David, the son of Jesse. Not long after David was anointed by Samuel. The Spirit of the LORD came upon him:

> *Then Samuel took the horn of oil, and anointed him in the midst of his brethren: and the Spirit of the LORD came upon David from that day forward. So Samuel rose up, and went to Ramah. I Samuel 16:13 [KJV]*

David was fierce and vigilant aggressively ready, and prepared to do battle with the giant on behalf of the soldiers who were afraid [I Samuel 17:24]of the giant. The name of the giant was Goliath. The soldiers were trained to engage in military battle. Nevertheless, David was trained to do battle with a giant. His resume and his track record went beyond military expertise. David was anointed by God. Therefore, he was more prepared than any ordinary soldier on the battlefield. His armor surpassed the armor of soldiers when Saul attempted to persuade him to dress, in the usual military attire David expressed the unproved amour may stand in this way of victory. David's amour is documented:

Finally, my brethren, be strong in the Lord, and in the power of his might. Put on the whole armour of God, that ye may be able to stand against the wiles of the devil. For we wrestle not against flesh and blood, but against principalities, against powers, against the rulers of the darkness of this world, against spiritual wickedness in high places. Wherefore take unto you the whole armour of God, that ye may be able to withstand in the evil day, and having done all, to stand. Stand therefore, having your loins girt about with truth, and having on the breastplate of righteousness; And your feet shod with the preparation of the gospel of peace; Above all, taking the shield of faith, wherewith ye shall be able to quench all the fiery darts of the wicked. And take the helmet of salvation, and the sword of the Spirit, which is the word of God: Praying always with all prayer and supplication in the Spirit, and watching thereunto with all perseverance and supplication for all saints; And for me, that utterance may be given unto me, that I may open my mouth boldly , to make known the mystery of the gospel. Ephesians 6:10-19 [KJV]

David was confident in his communication as he was engaged in communication with Saul:

Thy servant slew both the lion and the bear: and this uncircumcised Philistine shall be as of them, seeing he hath defied the armies of the living God. I Samuel 17:36 [KJV]

David convinced Saul that he was ready. Saul did not really get what David was saying, because Saul armed David with his amour:

And Saul armed David with his armour, and he put an helmet of brass upon his head; also he armed him with a coat of mail. And David girded his sword upon his armour, and he assayed to go; for he had not proved it. And David said unto Saul, I cannot go with these; for I have not proved them. And David put them off him. And he took his staff in his hand, and chose him five smooth stones out of the brook, and put them in a shepherd's bag which he had, even in a scrip: and his sling was in h is hand: and he drew near to the Philistine. I Samuel 17:38-40 [KJV]

So David prevailed over the Philistine with a sling and with a stone, and smote the Philistine, and slew him; but there was no sword in the hand of David. Therefore David ran, and stood upon the Philistine, and took his sword, and drew it out of the sheath thereof, and slew him, and cut off his head therewith, And when the Philistines saw their champion was dead they fled. I Samuel 17:50-51 [KJV]

When the Spirit of the LORD is upon a person or people you may notice the confidence, which is not to be compared to arrogance.

What the giant failed to realize he was looking at the Spirit of God housed inside of a ruddy young man godly to look to [I Samuel 16:12].

Likewise, people fail to understand the residing force of the Holy Ghost comforting, helping, and keeping the saints of God. You cannot see the Holy Ghost with your natural eyes because the power rest in the Spirit of God. We are not able to see electricity but when we turn the light switch on the light comes on. Therefore, we acknowledge; there is power, and we may use it or execute the power within.

When I reflect on Robert, I remember the first day I met him as I was driving down Stemmons Freeway to my professional printer. I remember the authoritative personality from a military officer conditioned to act with authority securing his target. It makes me smile to know that I met a fine military combat pilot. Recalling his communication to me when he asked me of my plans once the fashion show project was complete. I answered, saying, "I plan to take off for a vacation in Hawaii because I am exhausted." Robert paused looking into my eyes, saying with a confident flow of communication, asking, "How many will be in your company, Linda?" He was clever in his asking. "Just me," I answered. I felt like being a smart mouth saying, "Just Me, Robert."

He paused again, saying, "I am in the military, and I have been stationed in Hawaii twice. Hawaii is not the place for a single lady to travel alone. If you don't mind waiting until I complete my travel engagement, I would like to accompany you to protect you. The entire expense of the trip and travel is on me." Silently, I went into shock. Wondering was he for real or just some smooth talking gentlemen about to catch my sharp tongue of defense. The LORD helped me to keep my words soft and gentle. That Robert was from another caliber. I looked at him almost laughing and said, "Sure." Robert is a protector, and he was being his natural self. As we prepared to depart from each other because I was running behind schedule to meet with my printer. We exchanged business cards and he wrote two additional numbers on his card. One number was an international number where I could reach him anywhere in the world.

When it came time for Robert to be deployed, he did not back down, nor resist because he had just me. He answered the call of duty, saying, Lady. I will have to catch you later. I understood a little because of the incident surrounding the twin towers on September 11, 2001. What I did not understand when I learned that Robert was defending our county. The impact of 911 educated me. I prayed for Robert all the time. He is part of my adult college life. I take him everywhere I go. I pondered him in my heart for years not willing to talk about him to anyone. Because he was my hidden treasure:

And I will give thee the treasures of darkness, and hidden riches of secret places, that thou mayest know that I, the LORD, which call thee by thy name, am the God of Israel. Isaiah 45:3 [KJV]

When you find something precious and its stored it becomes a treasure. When you find it again, it becomes more precious than the day you first beheld. Familiar with the saying, "Set it was free, and if it returns to you, it belongs to you." With that being said, God can change his mind when he gets ready. He did not need the permission of people to do as he pleases. Realizing God is God and he can do as he pleases. I expect God's word to be manifest according to his will, purpose, and glory.

This is going to be interesting to see how God's glory is manifested. I know that God knows exactly what he is doing and all I need to do is follow the steps he had ordered for my life. It does not matter what people say about the fifteen years, the audible voice, and the dream that happened on January 16, 2011 because what God started, God is able to finish. Throughout the bible people spoke concerning a move of God without consulting with God. They faced his glory at the appointed time. My walk is secured in the LORD. I have a blessed church family and leadership, a blessed family, blessed friends, and blessed engagements with a truly blessed Pastor. I serve God, who is able.

I believe God hid Robert for an appointed day. Likewise, I believe Robert was also a catalyst to help me step into position to receive the blessing of a lifetime. A multitude is about to be touched and blessed according to God's appointed time. God did not waste his words, saying, "HE IS YOUR HUSBAND.' A rebirth of true love and solid marriage concrete and sealed in pure love is about to emerge. God used a soldier, and a combat pilot to awake my senses of my true calling an area of focus for multiple business endeavors. I watched God invested a word over Robert's life for his glory. And God and Robert know what may have been spoken by the audible voice of God, in Roberts's vehicle. It was no accident; it was a setup for an appointed time for God's glory. It seemed the longer a promised blessing is waited for the more powerful God's glory will shine.

Every time I read the story of David and think about Robert serving our country. I have a greater appreciation for our military personnel rather active or retired. I respect the sacrifice their families made and endured in their absence. Never seeing Robert attired in his military attired, I feel so proud seeing another soldier in passing fully arrayed. Passing by a military base, in Dallas, Texas, I see the military hummers and soldiers in passing. I have always respected them, but I respect and appreciate them more. I am able to often watch the military helicopters flying over my backyard. So many reminders of Robert salute me every day. I watch the news and I review events on the Internet sites of all the news surrounding the soldiers serving our great country. I read about the honor the White House provides and how the First Ladies are involved with the military families helping them to survive and manage their families.

Robert is currently fighting a giant, and he is not fighting the giant alone. I know the Spirit of the LORD is with him. There is about to be a shake and a shift on his behalf. God's appointed glory is not to be placed on hold. Pharaoh had no idea that he was about to face impending plagues because he refused to let the children of Israel go. They were serving under his rule, and he was treating them unjustly. Pharaoh did not understand a cry. When the children and saints of God cry out-God will send help. He will use one person, maybe two or more. Nevertheless, God will send a messenger to set his people free. There was a judge named Deborah, in the Bible. She was fierce in her position.

And Deborah said unto Barak, Up: for this is the day in which the LORD hath delivered Sisera into thine hand: is not the LORD gone out before thee? So Barak went down from mount Tabor, and ten thousand men after him. Judges 4:14 [KJV]

I am ready to listen. I am looking forward to hearing him, share the thrills of being a military aviation combat pilot. Especially while preparing to take my first flight on a jet, I have never flown on an airplane. This will be the perfect time for him to hold my hand, again. Knowing he is equipped with pilot skills to take over the flight with the Spirit of God. He might as well know the truth. Hoping to take my first flight seated next to him. I do believe God set this whole thing up knowing that Robert the man he introduced me to as my husband on the freeway may escort me on my first flight abroad a jet. I really hope to see him attired in his military attire for the first time. I hope to own my first Nikon 35mm and be ready, for the moment, because I am fascinated with photography.

Remembering he was the first gentleman who took me for a ride inside his brand new eighteen wheeler. Being horrified is an understatement. However, I felt I was in good hands with Robert doing the driving. Relaxing and listening to Robert sharing his military life will be a delight. I want to know if he too had dreams about me during those fifteen years. The story of David helped me to understand the being of Robert's life until I can hear him share his journey with me. The story of David fascinates me the most when I think of Robert because the Bible captures his life before he was anointed as the new king replacing Saul. The moment in history arrived when THE LORD spoke to Samuel, saying, I will send thee to Jesse the Bethlehemite: for I have provided me a king among his sons [I Samuel 16:16 KJV].

A WIFE FOR ISAAC

Whoso findeth a wife findeth a good thing, and obtaineth favour of the LORD.
Proverbs 18:22 [KJV]

I thought of all the elements of nature [trees, birds, animals, sea, seashore, sunshine, sky, earth, grass, water, wind, stars, sunset] and the wedding will take place outside at the Dallas Arboretum [which reminds me of the garden of Eden]. There is no other place I can imagine. The Reception and all will be at the Dallas Arboretum. Before the church edifices were built there was openness. Adam and Eve were united out in the openness of nature. Isaac and Rebekah, met out in the open as she rode to his destination with his father's eldest servant [Eliezer-Gen. 15:2] and with her damsels [Genesis 24:61]. Isaac and Rebekah met and married in the same day.

For she had said unto the servant, What man is this that walketh in the field to meet us? and the servant had said, It is my master: therefore she took a vail, and covered herself. Genesis 24:65 [KJV]

And the servant told Isaac all things that he had done. Genesis 24:66 [KJV]

And Isaac brought her into his mother Sarah's tent, and took Rebekah, and she became his wife; and he loved her: and Isaac was comforted after his mother's death. Genesis 24:67[KJV].

Understandably, the servant was a praying man, and his master Abraham provided specific instructions concerning the chosen wife for his son Isaac. Positive words spoken by Abraham were uttered saying:

The Lord God of heaven, which took me from my father's house, and from the land of my kindred, and which spake unto me, and that sware unto me, saying, Unto thy seed will I give this land; he shall send his angel before thee, and thou shalt take a wife unto my son from thence. Genesis 24:7[KJV]

Abraham remembered the history of his journey, which involved instructions from the LORD to *get thee out of thy country, and from thy kindred, and from thy father's house, unto a land that I will shew thee* [Genesis 12:1]. Abraham knew God was able and the LORD lead him all the way, for he was elevated as the father of nations. Leaving one familiar place to possess the promise land prepared with a provision. Abraham knew from experience to trust the LORD. Eliezer took ten camels of the camels of his master, and departed, and went to Mesopotamia, unto the city of Nahor [Genesis 24:10 KJV]. He went on a journey to find Isaac's wife. Eliezer settled the camels:

And he made his camels to kneel down without the city by a well of water at the time of the evening, even the time that women go out to draw water. And he said, O LORD God of my master Abraham, I pray thee, send me good speed this day, and shew kindness unto my master Abraham. [Genesis 24:12[KJV]

Eliezer put God first; he began his pursuit by having a talk with God to guide him that he might not make a mistake. Listen to his continual conversation with God:

And let it come to pass, that the damsel to whom I shall say, Let down thy pitcher, I pray thee, that I may drink; and she shall say, Drink, and I will give thy camels drink also: let the same be she that thou hast appointed for thy servant Isaac; and thereby shall I know that thou hast shewed kindness unto my master. Genesis 24:14[KJV]

Putting God first, is the same as purchasing a GPS System, an Atlas, and or a map to travel across the appointed destination but the guide is a divine map from God, a spiritual map if you will. Eliezer was on the right path:

And it came to pass, before he had done speaking, that, behold, Rebekah came out, who was born to Bethuel, son of Milcah, the wife of Nahor, Abraham's brother, with her pitcher upon her shoulder. And the damsel was very fair to look upon, a virgin, neither had any man known her: and she went down to the well, and filled her pitcher, and came up. Genesis 24:15-16 [KJV].

Attesting to the above scripture, praying to acknowledge a trust in God. We run to the source, trusting the Most High. Eliezer trusted God. Waking up from my dream [October 1998], I called Mother Jenkins, and after meeting Robert on the freeway, I called Mother Jenkins, but it was God, whom spoke to me with His audible voice not Mother Jenkins. I called the person I trusted over my trust in God. Mother Jenkins did not cause me to have the dream of being in the graveyard at midnight. The dream came from God. Growing into godly wisdom was essential to trust God more than I trusted people. Trusting a person just because they have a title, history of serving God, and knowledgeable on the Word of God, they may not be the appointed person to speak with concerning your dreams and supernatural experiences. It took me a long time to learn to go straight to God first, even if I have to journal my expressions. Acknowledging God first is putting God first. God was listening to the communication coming from Eliezer. Apparently, he was able to get a prayer request straight to God. The result of his prayer serves as validation to go to God in prayer [*prayer works*]:

And the servant ran to meet her, and said, Let me, I pray thee, drink a little water of thy pitcher. And she said, Drink, my lord: and she hasted, and let down her pitcher upon her hand, and gave him drink. And when she had done giving him drink, she said, I will draw water for thy camels also, until they have done drinking. And she hasted, and emptied her pitcher into the trough, and ran again unto the well to draw water, and drew for all his camels. [Genesis 24: 17-20 KJV]

His prayer was being answered:

And let it come to pass, that the damsel to whom I shall say, Let down thy pitcher, I pray thee, that I may drink; and she shall say, Drink, and I will give thy camels drink also: let the same be she that thou hast appointed for thy servant Isaac; and thereby shall I know that thou hast shewed kindness unto my master. [Genesis 24:14 KJV]

Noticing, the contents mentioned in verse 22 concerning the earring and the bracelets:

And it came to pass, as the camels had done drinking, that the man took a golden earring of half a shekel weight, and two bracelets for her hands of ten shekels weight of gold. [Genesis 24:22 KJV].

Adding, golden earring and the bracelets in the wedding ceremony program may be a highlight of how precious gold, which was mentioned from the beginning of time. Likewise, streets of gold are mentioned in the book of Revelation.

And the twelve gates were twelve pearls; every several gate was of one pearl: and the street of the city was pure gold, as it were transparent glass. [Revelation 21:21 KJV]

THE SACRED HUSBAND

*D*own through the years from a small child I watched couple interact with each other. It made my world to see a husband and wife greet each other with a kiss as the husband was coming in from work. That helped me to know that two people could be joyful being married. Every day I watched the couples in my neighborhood. They were under surveillance and they had no idea. My mind was made up. I desired a sacred husband who was loyal, loving, and caring. Having someone special to share my life, my day, and my joy was what I desired. Even so, I told God I desired a husband who could talk. The mature express is this, "God blessed me with a husband whom can effectively communication because you know I like to talk, right, and converse on various topics.

I knew if he read books his substance to communication may consist of a plethora of information. Reading a powerful book generates topics for conversation. God knew I also enjoyed my sabbatical time to reflect on my inner world to hear from God. I desired my husband to be one that traveled. I knew while my husband was home, he would have my undivided attention. Treating him like a king and helping him to eat healthy was my plan. He would always have his spa because I planned to pamper his feet once a week by filing his toe nails and removing any try skin before placing his feet into a thirty minute foot soak with a virgin coconut foot soak combined with a soothing peppermint.

Allowing the experience to mix. I would wrap his feet in plastic for ten minutes with the wrapping of warm towels around his feet.

Followed with warm almond oil massage, and a second message with Apricot nectar lotion. I study the structure of the feet to understand how to provide him the best benefits of a foot massage. Acknowledging that my husband will be the head of our home my plans are to respect his leadership completely. As long as he keeps the LORD as the head of his life. we together will be able to whether the storms of life an as well the blessings of holy matrimony.

For the husband is the head of the wife, even as Christ is the head of the church: and he is the savior of the body. Ephesians 5:23 [KJV]

Therefore as the church is subject unto Christ, so let the wives be to their own husbands in every thing. Ephesians 5:25 [KJV]

Husbands, love your wives, even as Christ also love the church, and gave himself for it; That he might sanctify and cleanse it with the washing of water by the word. Ephesians 5:25-26 [KJV]

That he might present it to himself a glorious church, not having spot, or wrinkle, or any such thing; but that it should be holy and without blemish. Ephesians 5:27 [KJV]

Submitting yourselves one to another in the fear of God. Ephesians 5:21 [KJV]

Wives, submit yourselves unto your own husbands, as unto the Lord. Ephesians 5:22 [KJV]

So ought men to love their wives as their own bodies. He that loveth his wife loveth himself. Ephesians 5:28 [KJV]

Nevertheless let every one of you in particular so love his wife even as himself; and the wife seet hat she reverence her husband. Ephesians 5:33 KJV]

As I grew and matured to read God's instructions, I am excited to showcase the following scripture to celebrate My Big Mama, Little

Mama, My Mother, and those twelve senior citizens for directing me with balance to understand life is not perfect. Therefore, we pray:

The aged women likewise that they be in behavior as becometh holiness, not false accusers, not given to much wine teachers of good things; that they may teach the young women to be sober, to love their husbands, to love their children. To be discreet, chaste, keepers at home, good, obedient to their own husbands, that the word of God be not blasphemed. Titus 2:2-5 [KJV]

PLANNING A WEDDING

*A*pril 8, 2011, appearing in my backyard near the exact location where Robert was standing three mountains blue birds appeared side-by-side looking down into the ground. Simultaneously, the thirty Garden Warblers appeared near the same location. On July 16, 2001, I drove to Bachman Lake with a heavy heart; Bible, journal, and a note pad. Spending time in the openness of nature has a way of soothing my soul surpassingly with peace, which the stress seems to exit my spirit. Seated at the table near the border of the lake by a huge and beautiful tree to my immediate right I started to write a few journal entries to empty the negatives of the early morning day. In the midst of writing at Bachman Lake, I occasionally paused to enjoy the easy flowing waters.

Writing for about twenty minutes I noticed the squirrel ran up into the tree, and another squirrel was going in and out of the waste can pausing for minute to my immediate left. The birds were flying low singing and tweeting as usual, and the airplanes were landing plus taking off. The collaboration of sounds played a natural musical chord of melody. It was enjoyable, and the surroundings was pleasantly dressed with green grass, ducks, and breathtaking trees. Something happened to me that day, which I did not understand so it's my custom to convert negatives experiences into positives results immediately. Especially after learning the danger of stress does to the internal body. I refuse to give a negative situation the stage over my life.

Upon my arrival, I noticed several people were walking their dogs, roller Some people were walking .and running for physical fitness benefits along with exercise. The scenery was tranquil and I started to embrace the sweet serenity of being outdoors at Bachman Lake. Over the years, I developed a personal fondness and passion for Bachman Lake. Near the end of my final journal entry, I noticed the sun started to shine extremely bright and the face of the waters had to transformation of millions of sparkling diamonds. It was a picturesque moment, but I was without a camera. I opened my bible to read scripture.

The sun expanded shining directly into my face, whereas I perceived to be odd because I was in a shaded location, but it appeared as if the sun found me to shine warmth on me. Expediently, the squirrel that was up in the tree stopping, moving and moved down the outer bark standing still looking at me. Then looking over to my left, the squirrel that was playing around in the waste can come up and stood at the same time at the top of the rim looking at me. Thinking what are they thinking and why are they both looking at me. Adding to the strange moment, two Ravens flew down out of the sky and stood at the edge of my opened bible. I sat there afraid to move because I had no idea. What could have possibly attracted them to me? Here comes the slow moving turtle. They came all the way up from the bank of the river and stood at attention at my left big toe. I had on open toe shoes. The squirrels made their way to the top of the table standing next to the ravens. They were looking at me, and I was wondering how to leave the table and run to my car. I did not know what to do. Since I own the movie called "The Birds," I was careful hoping they were not about to attack me.

Thinking silently, LORD. please make them go away. I heard people standing behind me that stopped in their tracks saying, "Look," "What do you make of that?" They went on and on making wondering remarks, I wanted someone to shew them away so I could run. The more the people stood obviously pointing in my direction. The more other people stood to watch. I thought of grabbing my bible to cover my face since all those people were looking, but several small children ran up and said, "Mommy look." They ran right upon me, and I wanted to hug them each. The birds and the squirrels started to leave the table, and I grabbed my belongings and ran as fast as could to my vehicle. I almost got a ticket I was driving so fast. It happened again at another lake. Finally, I learned that animals may often sense the presence of the LORD before human beings. I remember Balaam and the ass [Numbers 22:21-33. Noah used the raven [Genesis 8:6]. The LORD used two ravens [I Kings 17:4-6] to feed Elijah. The scripture concerning the ravens' interest me the most because the ravens were following instructions from God. Knowing could have sent angels to feed Elijah, but he used the ravens.

And it shall be, that thou shalt drink of the brook; and I have commanded the ravens to feed thee there. 1 Kings 17L4 [KJV]

And the ravens brought him bread and flesh in the morning, and bread and flesh in the evening; and he drank of the brook. 1 Kings 17:6 [KJV]

I read my academic books extensively being a full-time student studying psychology. The back porch is where I enjoy relaxing to read without interruptions. Besides I enjoy being in the midst of open nature. I have lived in this home for seven years, and I have never seen a raven or ravens stop and rest on the fence. Nor the roof tops of the homes behind me until after the dream on January 16, 2011. I keep my window open to watch the sunlight, weather, and sky as I am writing. It would be nice to live in a fine French or Mediterranean Luxury estate with options of writing on the Lanai. Balcony overlooking the pool, around the outdoor kitchen, and the outdoor veranda. Precisely, at the very moment, I could write from a cruise ship cruising, in Tahiti [Bora Bora], which is the exact locationof a day vision where I watched a cruise ship sailing southward. The vision came when I returned from visiting the Potter's House, in, I believe was August 1996. It happened about one week before I joined the Potter's House on September 1, 1996. I came in from worship service exhausted. I sat down on the edge of my bed, and I was facing the west. I closed my eyes as I normally do when I am exhausted. The moment I closed my eyes. I saw a large cruise liner sailing southward. My spirit was elevated above the thick green trees, and I could smell the water, and the trees. I opened my eyes and in disbelief. Closing my eyes for the second time, I saw the cruise ship sailing in the cool of the evening again. This time I said, "God, I will not be getting on that ship." The ship was huge. Opening my eyes for the third time, thinking of all that water, I said, "No way God I am not going to get on board of that cruise ship." I opened my eyes, I was laughing as I laid down to take a nap. I was already having an issue with flying.

If I were to plan a beautiful and simple outdoor wedding, the theme will be "**The Hundred Fold Wedding**" because the journey of life caused me to cry sometimes, many times:

And Jesus answered and said, Verily I say unto you, There is no man that hath left housed, or brethren, or sisters, or father, or mother, or wife, or children, or lands, for my sake and the gospel's. But he shall receive an hundredfold now in this time , houses, and brethren, and sisters, and mothers, and children, and lands, with persecutions; and in this world to come eternal life. But many that are first shall be last: and the last first. Mark 10:29-31 [KJV]

The wedding colors will be navy blue, pure white, and baby blue with a hint of scarlet red. The traditional wedding arch will be replaced with a replica of a large white framed window with triple thick trimmings. Similar to what I saw in the dream with Robert on January 16, 2011. The window would be decorated with pure white flowers with tall white bird cages for a Scarlet Tanager, three Mountains Blue Birds, Red Cardinal, and A Blue Jay with monarch butterflies shipped from the butterfly farm, which they will be set from immediately after the exchange of the wedding vows.

The wedding invitation will capture the same décor. I plan to keep the wedding ceremony simple and nice with greater hopes of giving God glory and thanks for speaking a word that helped me to live a righteous life. It was Manuel, a friend of my friend Gail, saying, and "God placed you inside a cocoon to protect you from the wrong man." He spoke those words to me on July 19, 2002, which was the same day I experience the encounter with a humongous butterfly that was as large as the size of my head, as soon as I arrived home and stepped out of my vehicle.

(As it is written, I have made thee a father of many nations,) before him WHOM HE BELIEVED, EVEN God, who quickeneth the dead, and

calleth those things which be not as though they were. Who against hope believed in hope, that he might become the father of many nations, according to that which was spoken, So shall thy seed be. Romans 4:17-18 [KJV]

IN THE beginning God created the heaven and the earth. And the earth was without form, and void; and darkness was upon the face of the deep. And the Spirit of God moved upon the face of the waters. And God said, Let there be light: and there was light. And God saw the light, that it was good: and God divided the light from the darkness. And God called the light Day, and the darkness he called Night. And the evening and the morning were the first day. Genesis 1:1-5 [KJV]

For 15/16 years, there was a void, darkness, and no form of a marriage but suddenly God reminded me of his spoken word on that day, in September 1995, HE IS YOUR HUSBAND

When God speaks a word from heaven into your life, and over your life keep these scriptures close to your heart with Faith, Trust, Obedience, and Determination to wait upon the LORD:

For my thoughts are not your thoughts, neither are your ways my ways, saith the LORD. For as the heavens are higher than the earth, so are my ways higher than your ways, and my thoughts than your thoughts. for as the rain cometh down, and the snow from heaven, and returneth [never have I seen the snow go in reserves up into the heavens, nor the rain-never seen drops of rain go into reserve back up into the heavens] not thither, but watereth the earth, and maketh it bring for and bud, that it may give seed to the sower, and bread to the eater: So shall my word be that goeth forth out of my mouth: it shall not return unto me void, but it shall accomplish that which I please, and it shall prosper in the thing whereto I sent it. Isaiah 55:8-11 [KJV]

Let people laugh, mock, plot, whisper, assume, and speak negative but you, hold on to God's word. God have a time when He will place your life on His Spiritual Stage and slowly pull back the Spiritual curtains and will cause his Glory to Shine. Your works and your weak moments where it seemed life was unbearable from all the lies, plots, pits, and attacks. God allowed you to stand in the weak position to expose your enemies to set the stage for his glory. He allowed them to oppress you, and laugh you to scorn for a little while. All God needed was a little while of your time to set-the-stage for his glory. You endured for His Glory and now come the rewards from heaven. You can point all your enemies out, but God instructed you to:

But I say unto you, Love your enemies, bless them that curse you, do good to them that hate you, and pray for them which despitefully use you, and persecute you. That ye may be the children of your Father which is in heaven; for he maketh this sun to rise on the evil and on the good, and sendeth rain on the just and on the unjust. For if ye love them which love you, what reward have ye? do not even the publicans the same? Matthew 5:44-46 [KJV]

God spoke out-in-the openness of a condition, and He changed the three negative elements by speaking into the circumstances. A wedding conducted in open nature is accompanied with a decorated day and sky appointed by God, which all things were created by God from the beginning of time. I think of wedding plans and I change my plans ocassionally.On God will arrange the colors of the sky according to his plan and purpose. The wedding may take place outside at the Dallas Arboretum, which reminds me of the garden of Eden. There is no other place I can imagine more suitable, since Robert, and I met in the openness on the freeway. Plus we spoke for more than eight hours outside at the park across the street from my condominium holding hands. The wedding reception and all to follow may be will be held at the Dallas Arboretum or the courthouse. It really does not matter. It's fund thinking about wedding plans. .

The minister conducting the officiating of the covenant wedding vows will be of Robert's choice. Before a church buildings/edifices were constructed the church, there was the waters. Accentuating the wedding will be the view of White Rock Lake. There is no other place I can imagine more fitting than the Dallas Arboretum. The Reception and all will evolve at the Dallas Arboretum. Adam and Eve were united out in the openness of nature. Isaac and Rebekah, met out in the open as she rode to his destination with his father's eldest servant [Eliezer-Gen. 15:2] and with her damsels [Genesis 24:61]. Isaac and Rebekah met and married in the same day.

he foolish. A married that sleeps around with other women is absent of the dwelling of the Holy Spirit, which caused me to think of a reprobate mind:

And even as they did not like to retain God in their knowledge, God gave them over to a reprobate mind, to do those things which are not convenient. Romans 1:28 [KJV]

Now as Jannes and Jambres withstood Moses, so do these also resist the truth: men of corrupt minds, reprobate concerning the faith. 2 Timothy 3:8 [KJV]

They profess that they know God; but in works they deny him, being abominable, and disobedient, and unto every good work reprobate. Titus 1:16 [KVJ]

I disagree with excuses from the flesh ruling because God is a spirit and he is not weak. He is without limits, and he is Holy. Serving God means we serve one true God. You can not serve two masters:

No man can serve two masters: for either he will hate the one, and love the other; or else he will hold to the one, and despise the other. Ye cannot serve God and mammon. Matthew 6:24 (Luke 16:13) [KJV]

THE BUTTERFLY ENCOUNTER

I came personally face-to-face with the largest butterfly in the world. On July 19, 2002. I had just returned from visiting Gail's home to meet and witness to Jaciee. Manual was there visiting Gail, and he asked me to take the seat. He was featured on a popular radio station with a large audience. He asked me to take a seat, while I was waiting on Jaciee. The first thing he said to me was, "Stop wearing so much black, and change your colors to vibrant light colors." I looked at him waiting for the next message. He was firm, bold, and confident, whereas he never blinked to doubt this communication, which is what held my interest.

If I sense you are flaky, weak, or nervous, when talking to me-I will detach from your communication. Nevertheless, this gentleman, held my interest. Normally, I will prevent you from approaching me-but he captured my essence, which allowed me to receive his communication. He was a conscious gentleman. He was not afraid of me, because I will give off the air as unapproachable. Manual spoke so much information to me concerning my life, which Gail, had no knowledge. Even so, the one thing, which stood out was when Manual saying, "God placed you inside a cocoon to protect you from men, the wrong men." Driving home, I examined his conversation and especially the part where he said, "God placed me inside of a cocoon to protect me from the wrong me."

When I drove into the property of my condo [Westmount] I parked the car. When I came close to the outside stairs, this HUGE HUMONGOUS butterfly appeared to come from the southwest dancing with grace right in my face. I stood still trying to embrace the colors and the size. The butterfly danced for nearly five-minutes. Suddenly tears came rolling down my cheeks as if something broke loose from off my life. The large butterfly started flying backwards never breaking contact. I turned slowly to watch in total disbelief. Continuing to watch the butterfly until it flew backwards out of my sight heading north. As soon as the butterfly was out of sight I ran up my outdoor stars to log on to my computer. I wanted to know the exact name of that great big butterfly. It was big as my head. I thought for years it was the Swallowtail Butterfly. Then this year [2011], I learned the swallowtail was not the butterfly, whereas it is not as big as my big head. It was the male version of the Queen Alexandria. I talked about that butterfly until Mrs. Jewel K. oil painted me a swallowtail butterfly. I need to call her and tell her she may need to paint me another one but of the male version of the largest butterfly in the world. She and I worked together at the energy company.

ONLY GOD KNOWS

Robert's natural propensity to be kind, gentle, and attentive was illustrated to me on the freeway September 1995. His cosset nature to nurture the woman he loves was easy to recognize even in the short time I spent time with him and talked over the telephone long distance. He is not afraid to open his heart to the right woman. He is comfortable with himself not willing to take orders or get permission to love from anyone except God and his heart.

Out of all the gentlemen, I have met from the first time I went on a date, I never had one to flag me down on the freeway, but I would have missed him if it had not been for the audible voice of God-I probably would not have looked over to my right. I remember driving upon the freeway with great speed, pushing the music into the radio, and turning up the volume to hear the first tune, which was interrupted with the sound of the audible voice of God. A man can easily identify his own essence in the woman housing his spiritual DNA. When God established the appointed time for us to meet for the first time-God selected Stemmons Freeway of all places. It was stated that a man enjoys the pursuit-God allowed Robert to execute his bold and aggressive pursuit to meet his essence.

A Masterpiece Marriage was being constructed and processed for a Masterpiece Wedding Ceremony. Which I am inclined to hire a professional artist to paint the altar of marriage during the wedding ceremony. One thing for sure I felt safe being in the midst of Robert the first time I met him. The second we met, I felt the same protection. The next three visits he made to see me where at my mom's home, which was the last place I saw and spoke to Robert face-to-face. The people watching Noah build the ark, which they probably thought he was, derange all-the-way en-sane but when the flood came it was too late to believe the spoken word of God to Noah. God is on display of His spoken word from September 1995. I was chosen, and Robert was chosen all for God's glory. I do not know the current martial or status of Robert. It was God that allowed me to see him in a dream on January 16, 2011, wearing very familiar clothing of something I know very well. This marriage union is ordained with the master's touch.

The 100 Soldier Military Sword may compliment the wedding them and Robert's dedication to serving in the military. There's a significant meaning surrounding the 100 Soldier Military salute and possibly a one-hundred minister nucleus circle of prayer surrounding the entire wedding ceremony. I have so many creative ideas for my ceremony.

God established a provision for me to meet Robert, before the foundations of the world. A wedding you may witness is deemed to be an unprecedented ceremony. A ready order of a fifty monarch butterfly release after the exchange of the covenant marriage vows. Thereafter, the release of white doves. I believe the doves should be released at the moment the bride and groom leaves the altar announced as husband and wife. The doves fly away together, and likewise, the newly married husband and wife walk away from the altar holding hands. It sounds so lovely.

My wedding colors will be navy blue and pure white reflective of the colors Robert was wearing in the dream on January 16, 2011. The bridal bouquet will be scarlet red roses shipped in fresh to Cebolla Fine Flowers. The sky is a sapphire blue at night and a nice mild blue during the day with pure white clouds. The wedding reception will be administered in the fine fashion at an exclusive hotel ballroom with fine white linen table cloths.

My Big Mama, love to sing, "I Shall Not Be Moved," while preparing dinner. Without question, one will sing My Big Mama's favorite song during the wedding and the wedding reception.

WRESTLING

As the days pass by and time turned into years, I wrestled with all the dreams, and the memory of that precise moment when I heard the audible voice of God saying, HE IS YOUR HUSBAND. Those words are etched in my memory, and they will not go away. Within the dreams of seeing a tall slender, preppy, the athletic gentleman, I could see him clearly in the dreams but waking up the defined memory of his face would fade. Perhaps it was God's way of guiding me to remember. When a tall slender gentleman of caliber and style would approach me my first thoughts were of Robert. His approach on the freeway was different and unexpected,

The moment I looked to the right seeing him with all his lawful force beckoning me to pull over as if he knew me. It was not the kind of approach a man would use when meeting a stranger. It was the approach of a couple that were married, and he spotted her on the freeway and demanded that she pull over. As I am typing the memory is being celebrated in my thoughts. After experiencing the dream on January 16, 2011, I felt compelled to drive to the exact location where we first met. The memory comes to life each time I place that location and no matter how busy the flow of traffic my thoughts rush back in time, and I remember Robert's long walk to my vehicle. Everything about him is authority, confidence, and I have never been so mesmerized by anyone in my entire life.

Standing over my vehicle looking into my window, saying, "I apologize for that scene on the freeway with a sincere smile. He must have caught a glance of my perplexed expression trying to decipher the announcement from God, and looking over to see this very handsome gentleman aggressively boldly demanding for me to pull over immediately. Retrospectively, his actions on the freeway had to be prompted by the audible voice of God, perhaps I was not the only one that heard the audible voice. Surely, Robert is very much involved in an intimate relationship and communications with God.

No one can sing with such as anointing and not have the dwelling of the power of the Holy Ghost. Most men will look at you and walk up to you with the suave approach and say, "Hello my name is Robert. I could not help but to notice you. Do you mind if we talk for a few minutes?" That is the normal kind of approach I encountered. However, with Robert's his approach was peremptorily with urgency. When you let go of what you thought was from God to receive the truth blessings from God, it might cost you some time, and on the other hand, it may not. The greater the misery, the greater the blessing. There might be a sermon out there with that title, if not someone needs to preach that message. If I were a minister I might talk first about time speaking around the time journey of Joseph covering his double dreams to the day of fruition. The children of Israel that suffered awhile, and because of their sufferings in Egypt under the bondage of Pharaoh, at the appointed time, God parted the Red Sea for them to cross.

God's glory was on parade not the glory of men. Speaking of scripture according to time, waiting, and finally the promise. The promise land took time to acquire. The building of the ark by Noah took time to construct. When God speaks a word. However, he speaks through dreams, visions, small still voice, audible voice, and supernatural visitation it causes a shake and a shift. His word will never fail, which the best example in the beginning of the Bible when His Spirit moved over the face of the waters saying, Let there be light. The elements of a void, no form, and darkness had to be transformed for the manifestation of light. His voice is dependable and with all authority to bring forth the manifestation of whatever he speaks. It might seem foolish to man but there is a word recorded to bring light to foolishness:

For the wisdom of this world is foolishness with God. For it is written, He taketh the wise in their own craftiness. And again, The Lord knoweth the thoughts of the wise, that they are vain. Therefore let no man glory in men. For all things are yours. I Corinthians 3:19-21 [KJV]

But God hath chosen the foolish things of the world to confound the wise; and God hath chosen the weak things of the world to confound the things which are mighty. 1 Corinthians 1:27 [KJV]

God's word cannot and will not fail. Sincerely, I thought Robert was pointing out that something was wrong with my vehicle. Even so, God was speaking to me concerning Robert. I wrestled with so many thoughts at that instance. Plus I was talking back to God, saying, "I know you are not talking about the one I just dropped." Robert, probably saw me moving my mouth thinking I was going to yell at him taking an urgent compelling approach for me to pull over. All these years I never thought perhaps his aggressive and sudden approach was because he too heard the audible voice of God. And we both thought not to share the experience of hearing the audible voice not knowing if the other person was spiritually prepared/mature with knowledge of the supernatural move of God here on earth. We witness the sun rising but when we hear the sound of his voice, our thoughts change, and we try to separate the power of God into a category. The sun is yet shining [Genesis 1:16], and I believe God is continually speaking. I am glad that God created all things [Ephesians 3:9 & Genesis 1:26]. Evidently, Robert must be a praying man, which was obvious after hearing him sing that gospel song to me. He first looked up into the sky after asking my permission to sing to me. Then he looked deep into my eyes, and he started singing like a hosts of heavenly angels in one voice. Surely, my countenance started to unfold right before his eyes. Actually, I was waiting to laugh if he sounded awful; pondering the thought he must be with a humorous nature and desired to make me laugh. He is truly blessed by God with vocal abilities to sing around the throne in heaven. I know and have heard powerfully anointed singers, but I have never heard anyone sing above Robert's ability.

If I were to actually marry him, he will be singing at picnics we share by the lake. Our picnic time is called "The Quintessential Picnic', which is the name of my live radio talk show on Blog Talk Radio. Meeting Robert out in the openness of nature enhanced my appreciation for the outdoors, especially an outdoor picnic by the lake.

I may need to prepare for a custom tailor made the picnic blanket with the theme "The Quintessential Picnic embroidered as a monogram with our first and last names in the center or right hand corner. The likeness of "The Quintessential Picnic" Picnic Basket with a bronze name tag monogrammed with our first names. I look forward to hearing Robert's share so many things with me seated on the picnic blanket by the lake, on the seashore, in the backyard picnic. I am ready to hear the sound of his voice. I do not care if he talks from sun up to sun down because I am sure I will be encouraging him to write a book about me.

It was the way Robert was looking at me, as if he never wanted to remove his eyes off me. I too never wanted him to leave me nor remove his eyes' contact. It felt as if a transfusion of my spirit was connecting to my soul-mate. He was so kind, caring, and sincere without me having to play the guessing game. However, in the back of my mind I was asking questions of my silent self on the freeway, "Is this man for real? This cannot be real? Actually, as I am wrestling over the memory of the first encounter so many things are coming back to my memory that I have ignored all these fifteen years. The gentleman with the king mindset, which I have always desired was standing before me. God knows me, if he did not point the man out I will remain single for the rest of my life. The last date was proof that I needed the LORD to help me. Learning that many marriages are arranged by the parents, in particular, cultures, I can handle the perspective of an arranged marriage providing it is ordained and spiritually joined by God. I was wrestling with the thoughts of how Abraham sent is the eldest servant to search for a wife for his son Isaac. His servant was a praying man. He inquired of the LORD to guide him. Today, I wrestle with so much thought of that day on Stemmons Freeway when I met Robert. Life was so busy and I did not have time to think I was always rushing because my plate was full with things to do without delay. Even so, God interrupted my business to introduce me to Robert.

There are so many things that we learn to late about a mate that would have helped us save precious time. No godly woman wants to date a man who is a liar, cheat, and a womanizer. Especially not this woman, I have always desired a man with the mind of a king. Most people that really know me are aware that the classic Cinderella movie

[Rodgers & Hammerstein's Cinderella] is my favorite movie in this world. It is the first and only movie I watched with both my grannies, and I spent the night because I was not allowed to go outside after dark. My grannies prepared for me to watch the movie without interruptions. I would sing along with the cast, every song and my favorite song in the movie is "Ten Minutes Ago." That song means so much to me. The classic Cinderella movie came on each year, and I have my very own copy to watch on the fourth of July, which is how I celebrate My Big Mama's Birthday and with all the planned display of fireworks. It completes my day of celebration remembering the joy the three of us shared watching Cinderella movie together is a sweet reflection. Plus I had full access to any leftover's which was seldom but my grannies made sure I had plenty to eat.

I sat directly in front of the television set about three feet centered. No one moved or spoke one word while the movie was on. I love the way the prince approach Cinderella, and foremost how he disallowed her step mother to be mean to hear. Nevertheless, when he looked into her eyes singing all those beautiful words my heart slowly melted every time. While writing this portion of the manuscript, I am reminded that Robert stood before me outdoors singing a gospel song. He first asked my permission if he could.

Sing to me. This must have been his approach on stage and tour, being that he informed me that he was formerly with a member of a professional gospel recording group. He took control of every situation, yes; Robert is a take charge kind of a gentleman. He presents a plan that was difficult to refuse. I am yet amazed and thankful to God for allowing me to hear his audible voice. I am glad I had the opportunity and the privilege of meeting Robert. Once quick glance at Robert was a moment to frame in my memory for ever. Stemmons Freeway will never be the same for me. His first repeated words were "Pull Over!" God allowed me to look to my right to take notice of Robert's repeated gesture demanding immediate action of a woman that knew him as a stranger. I have wrestled with the possible reason of his approach. I believe Robert would have followed me all the way to my printer-. I just believe One thin and with him not knowing the real reason why I suddenly slammed on my breaks he probably felt he best apologize before I ruined the moment with the wrong tone and words. So many thoughts were activated in my mind after hearing the audible voice of God. And I have wrestled with the words spoken by the audible voice concerning Robert for the past fifteen years. The dreams and visions kept him alive in my heart. So I never dated anyone but there is one man who may come close to Robert, but I will ponder his name. He is the only man. I know that may come close, but we have never dated.

And Jacob was left alone; and there wrestled a man with him until the breaking of the day. And when he saw that he prevailed not against him, he touched the hollow of his thigh; and the hollow of Jacob's thigh was out of joint, as he wrestled with him. And he said, let me go, for the day breaketh. And he said, I will not let thee go, except thou bless me. And he said unto him, What is thy name? And he said, Jacob. And he said, Thy name shall be called no more Jacob, but Israel: for as a prince hast thou power with God and with men, and hast prevailed. And Jacob asked him, sand said, Tell me, I pray thee, thy name. And he said, Wherefore is it that thou dost ask after my name? And he blessed him there. And Jacob called the name f the place Peniel: for I have seen God face to face, and my life is preserved. And as he passed over Penuel the sun rose upon him, and he halted upon his thigh. Genesis 32:24-31 [KJV]

STAND FAST therefore in the liberty wherewith Christ hath made us free, and be not entangled again with the yoke of bondage. Galatians 5:1 [KJV]

Everything in my life was hurting me deeply when I heard the audible voice reading the scriptures off the page of the bible. I stopped reading and sat there on the edge of my bed looking at my bible amazed. I knew no one would believe me, so I called no one. All I knew to do was call upon the name of the LORD. When I met Robert the second time, he drove to my condo, driving the brand new rig, which he said on the freeway [September 1995] that he had purchased, and he was short of a driver. I had never stood so near a rig. It was almost frightening reminding me of an airplane,

DECEMBER 1995

*R*eading the story of Joseph over and over helped me to really understand that God's time is different from the time frame we set for things to happen. Yes, we are made in his image and in his likeness but his thoughts are higher:

For my thoughts are not your thoughts, neither are your ways my ways, saith the LORD. For as the heavens are higher than the earth, so are my ways higher than your ways, and my thoughts than your thoughts. Isaiah 55:8-9 [KJV]

It took Joseph thirteen years to experience the fruition of the double dreams at age seventeen. His father Israel [Jacob] the patriarch was given a false report concerning the possible death of this son Joseph by his sons. I wondered why God allowed Israel to believe the strategically prepared false report. God allowed for Israel to live for years thinking his son Joseph was killed. One day while attending the Potter's House, I heard Pastor T. D. Jakes preach a message concerning God's glory and another message concerning the things that happen in life. For eleven years, I listened as a member to countless sermons with profound messages, which was life changing.

Every time he opened his mouth I was empowered to think higher than on the surface. He taught me how to think outside of a boxed and to think beyond the voices of other people that were thinking from the same box with limited insight and experiences. There was more information waiting for me to research and investigate. Having an inquisitive nature to understand the beginning, root, and what makes everything work. I knew I was under the appointed leadership for preparation. Pastor Jakes taught me the meaning of the Holy Spirit

[Holy Ghost Anointing]. It was more to the Holy Spirit than two words spoken and read repeatedly from pastors, minister, and church leaders. It was important for me to know the power of the Holy Ghost.

One day I was invited to attend the Potter's House, which I was already a member of another mega church located in Dallas, Texas. Apparently, it was time for the shift. I was about to experience a dimensional shift, which required dimensional preaching from the Spirit of God. I was learning the knowledge through extensive Biblical studies at my current church. Attending the Potter's House may be considered the Harvard Biblical School of the anointing. The young lady who invited me to attend the Potter's House telephoned me one minute after I experienced a supernatural visitation, in my bedroom at my mother's home.

It happened around July 1996. I was typing up a sermon, which is one of my hobbies. Suddenly, a deep urgent sleep came over me. With the Wheel writer typewriter on the west side of my bed, I stopped typing the sermon to go to bed. As soon as I turned off the lights and closed my eyes, I felt a presence in the room. Standing near the other side of the typewriter was a man dressed in a black suit without the traditional collar. His shoes were black and his eyes were stern almost squished closed. Positioned around his image was a shining bright light which lit up my room. His right hand palm side up was extended over my typewriter over the top of my opened bible. It was as the invitation. I was trying to figure who the person was which he looked similar to the gentleman who was preaching on the VHS recording titled "Chosen."

The young lady who invited me let view the tape. When I first glanced at the VHS at her home, the title stood out over all the tapes in her case. I watched that video probably over fifty times because I wanted to hear every word over and over. I heard him mention a reason why I encountered all those attacks, and I wanted to hear it over and over. It felt as if someone understood my life, and I had never met Pastor Jakes. Looking at the image in my room under the bright light I desperately tried to recognize the person which it looked like my deceased father, gentleman friend, and also the man in the VSH tape. Looking up and down the image I screamed because it was not a natural person with flesh. It was like a glorified body or one transparent. I had seen something similar with My Big Mama, on July 10, 1971.

I stopped trying to figure who it was, and I started screaming to the top of my lungs, and I felt my tummy spit open. I screamed loud three times and when I jumped up to run out the room the hand took hold of the door knob, but I refused to remain in that room. I pulled the door open with such a force until it hit my forehead really hard–that hurt. The whole neighborhood was inside my mother's hallway standing at my bedroom door. One person said, "We heard you screaming all the way down the street." The next comments came from my baby son, saying, "My Mommy must have seen a rat." No way, I was going to share with them what just happened, and they were waiting with silence but I said, "I am OK" closing the door. As soon as I sat on the edge of the bed the telephone ring. It was the young lady calling to invite me to the Potter's House, saying, "The LORD told me to invite you to visit the Potter's House." I told her, "No thank you. I have heard about the running, shouting, and speaking in tongues. "I shared with her what happened in my room, and she quickly gave an answer without praying so I dismissed her comments.

She insisted that I attend her church, so we reached a compromise. She attended my church morning worship service, and she cooked a feast of greens, candy yams, cornbread and chicken and dressing with several cakes and pies, so I would be at her home to not be able to back out. When we arrived at the Potter's House we had to stand outside for hours. I took off my shoes, and I was standing at the doors with a multitude of people looking at her wondering why I allowed her to visit the Potter's House. When they finally opened the doors, she took off running, as if she was running track. I put my shoes on and laughed all the way inside watching people run to seats. It was my first experience to see people running into the church. Surely, this was a significant place.

She saved me, a seat, and I looked upside her head and I laughed within remembering how fast she took off running into the church. When Pastor Jakes and his wife Serita came out walking across the pulpit I froze. He was wearing the exact black suit and shoes from the supernatural visitation. When he stood resting on his left arm on the pulpit desk/lectern he slowly raised his right arm with the palm upward and spoke about two words.

Every person seated in the sanctuary ran to the aisle shouting. I was the only person seated. Pastor Jakes was now standing on the altar as the people were in the aisle shouting. This was an emergency. I spoke to God within, saying, "LORD, you know I dislike ministers touching me and make me fall. Do not let him touch me because I will be walking over these pews. You know I will do it. If I can't walk over them, I will crawl beneath until I reach the front door."

He looked at me eye-to-eye, and he closed his eyes shouting with a loud voice, saying, "I am the shepherd my sheep know my voice." My body rose up from the pew without my permission. John chapter ten was the chapter I studied at work on that passed Friday during lunch. During Bible study, I had spoken to my coworker sharing that it was one of my favorite chapters because it reminded me of the following scripture:

The last time I saw Robert face-to-face was in December 1995. It seems that God lead me to the Potter's House to learn about the Power of the anointing. Plus Pastor Jakes talked a lot about living a holy lifestyle. I found out that the Holy Ghost is a keeper. As people we will face temptation but when the Holy Ghost is operating in your life you learn the value of surrendering your flesh under the subjection of the Holy Ghost.

You learn the value of a priceless and precious diamond on display that is not to be touched by everybody. Only a limited few will be able to behold the beauty of a kept diamond. The same goes for those beautiful cultured pearls:

Give not that which is holy unto the dogs, neither cast ye your pearls before swine, lesy they trample them under their feet, and turn again and rend you. Matthew 7:6 [KJV]

"I DID THIS FOR YOU"

*F*ifteen years is a long time to journey pondering audible communication spoken by God. I can try to interpret the dream from January 16, 2011, or I can wait on the LORD to reveal the true meaning of the dream. It seems that in my weakest moments God does something amazing to refresh my journey. The dream happened late Sunday evening. It was an evening where I felt so hurt so I prayed and went to bed early. Deep into my sleep I felt the actual presence of someone in my room. I opened my eyes to see the visual vision of an isolated thick white framed window appearing about twelve inches from my bedroom window. The man in the window was Robert, the military aviation pilot. My eyes opened between the dream and the vision. He called out my name saying, "Linda come outside." Those were the exact words he spoke to me the second time he was in Dallas, Texas and he came to visit me, whereas I was living in my condo. He said, "Linda come outside."

Drifting back into the dream, I jumped up running to the back door, and I ran outside. There was Robert standing near the window six feet away. He was standing in the same location where the Jet exploded over the backyard with the rope/lasso was around the front of the Jet, and the other end was still in my hand. This was also a dream that happened on February 13, 2006. I jumped up so high to greet him, but he had this phlegmatic disposition waiting for me to be still and pay attention. I finally stood still at the same time looking up into his eyes. He then pointed to the south with his left hand saying, "I DID THIS FOR YOU." A beautiful estate appeared, and it was breathtaking. I was more excited about seeing Robert than the estate. I started dancing with excitement again and this time he finally smiles.

For some reason, he wanted me to see the estate, and he called me, outside so I could see what he wanted me to see. He was later relaxed and excited to see me. I woke up out of the dream. Robert and when I finally calmed down and stood still he said, Shoe me your feet. I pulled the sock off my right foot and expose my red toe nail polished with excitement. we both started laughing, and I woke up. He was wearing a navy blue sports jacket, navy blue designer shirt with then white stripes, and navy blue designer slacks. Robert is very tall over me, so I was always looking up into his eyes. His clothing looked familiar, and the words he spoke were familiar with another dream and actual real experience but with a pastor I know, which appeared in my dream speaking those same words and speaking them to my actual face, whereas it was face-to-face.

Calling Karen to share the dream, she mentioned who she thought it was but the gentleman was Robert. However, the clothing was that of another, which I had recently witness being worn three consecutive days in a row. I knew the other elements were not to be ignored, but I willingly decided to ignore the details. Remembering the pain that caused me to feel so weak I focused on why I was seeing Robert after all these years. I am not sure of the meaning of the number fifteen and the number sixteen, but it's been a long time since I felt covered, protected, and celebrated by a man. The last time I felt that kind of protection was on Stemmons Freeway when I met Robert. She silenced her words to avoid a disagreement because she was adamant thinking it was the other person. She said, "Robert is releasing you to marry." I refused to believe her words, so I ended the conversation to return to my sleep. I prayed again and went back to sleep, and I slept peacefully.

I believe I had to learn patience and to get rid of things I have carried hidden under a bright smile and soothing laughter and pleasant conversation. Most of us have encountered negative things and negative people in life. Therefore, we arm ourselves with blocks to prevent people from hurting us, and we refuse to reside and stay connected to those that continually inflict us with pain. We seek the joyful people and joyful surrounding that elevate the joy that God gave us. God carried me and protected me until I was ready for my husband, and my husband was now prepared and ready for me. Thinking about the last time I saw Robert, which was in December 1995.

Remembering, Robert's right lazy eye [Amblyopia], which was the one thing I noticed the most-right after he mentioned to me that he was a military aviation combat pilot and being deployed to Bosnia. It was not that noticeable, but I zoomed into his right eye on the last night. I saw him. Often times when we were together I was seated on his right side, and he was driving but that night as we starred at each other for hours saying nothing, I noticed the condition of his right eye. I stared at Robert seated in that chair trying to paint a mental portrait because my camera was in my storage unit and there was no time to make plans to take the additional pictures. I wanted to remember him with my mind mentally.

Robert was in a class all by himself, and I liked everything about him, including his imperfections and the pain he shared with me with tears rolling down his cheeks-he mattered to me. It was difficult to understand why God spoke, saying, HE IS YOUR HUSBAND, and then allowed Robert to be deployed to Bosnia. We never had time to really date. Walking with him outside to his vehicle, I watched him slowly drive away heading west. I watched him until he turned to the left out of my view. The massive flood of dreams started about three days after he left bound for his deployment to Bosnia. I knew he was involved in training to take to the skies again for combat. Not understanding the critical nature of his deployment, I was disappointed that he was now on the other side of the world far away from me. Near the end of October 1998, I moved back into the exact condominium #229. I placed his information in the top drawer of my night stand to keep him close. When I got ready to move into his home, the package of information was missing. Either someone removed it without my knowledge, or it was accidentally removed. I have searched and searched for the cassette recording after the dream on January 16, 2011. Each time the news media broadcast that a pilot was shot down in Bosnia my hopes of seeing Robert started to vanish. He told me that his mother would contact me if anything were to happen to him.

Neither Robert nor I realized that all of my telephone numbers would change including my address. Life was so busy and I failed to ask the right questions of Robert with him being in a mental zone thinking about the outcome of his life. I lost all the information Robert gave to me, including his long distance telephone numbers, the personal cassette recording he made for me to listen to, which I never had the chance to listen all the way through because of the noise at the beginning, and I was always busy or distracted. He told me if anything happened to him in Bosnia, that his mother would contact me. My heart dropped to the floor and shattered into so my pieces. Life had already flipped and then he was deployed.

I believe God is telling me that Robert is alive. Additional dreams led me to an article online which when I read the article, and I knew that was Robert is alive. Remembering he told me that he had been stationed in Hawaii twice as a military soldier. He never shared with me that he was a pilot until he received notice of possible deployment. It yet did not register with me the seriousness surrounding military life less known being a combat pilot. I watched westerns but one day I watched the movie titled "Pearl Harbor" with actor Ben Affleck. I purchased the movie, and I have my own personal copy. It helped me to understand what Robert may have felt being a combat pilot, in the military.

After the dream on January 16, 2011, I decided to go ahead and write the book titled "HE IS YOUR HUSBAND," which are the exact words spoken by the audible voice of God on that particular day in September 1995. A lady from a popular Internet site also inspired me to write this book. Robert was wearing a navy blue sports jacket, with a navy blue designer shirt with thin white strips. He was inside an isolated thick white framed window. I was sleep but having a dream, but I felt his spirit fill my room and looking at the frame from a dream to a live vision he said, "Linda, come out side." In the dream, I jumped up running so fast until I did not remember my feet touching the floor, but I ran very fast into my back yard. I have wrestled with this matter for fifteen years, and soon to be sixteen come September 2011.

Reconciliation, Reconstruction, and Restoration, is established once the foundation of building the purpose for the future is complete. When your foundation is solid as concrete you are able to stand without wavering. Years ago, I was not ready for marriage. I may have thought I was ready, but I really was not prepared for the man who God appointed to be my husband because I was silently broken and I hid the hurt with a ready smile. If something hurt me and pierced me, I walked away thinking I was protecting me but never standing up and talking it over and sometimes waiting to talk it over will cause much delay. I was carrying hidden luggage without realizing my future was forced to wait for the emptied space. Through it all I learned people and how to protect my close inner circle. The things that God promised me he had to hold back until I was ready for the blessings. It was important for me to learn the difference of the heart of a person versus actions. I learned patience, endurance, how to wait upon the LORD, and how to trust the LORD with my whole heart. Walking through and out of the negative experiences, which I refuse to write about because it's time to walk in God's promises and purpose to give him glory. My life is now a solution.

I grew up sheltered and naïve and the price of learning was painful, hurtful, and deeply felt to the comfort of tears releasing portions of the blows. A tree endures the weather and storms but that tree that is not securely planted. They are damaged and often uprooted. Finding comfort today, in the following scriptures:

She is more precious than rubies: and all the tings thou canst desire are not to be compared unto her. Length of days is in her right hand; and in her left hand riches and honour. He ways are ways of pleasantness, and all her paths are peace. She is a tree of life to them that lay hold upon her: and happy is every one that retaineth her. The LORD by wisdom hath founded the earth; by understanding hath he established the heavens. By his knowledge the depths are broken up, and the clouds drop down the dew. Proverbs 3:15-20 [KJV]

Then shalt thou walk in thy way safely, and why foot shall not stumble. When thou liest down thou shalt not be afraid: yea thou shalt lie down, and thy sleep shall be sweet. Be not afraid of sudden fear, neither of the desolation of the wicked, when it cometh, For the LORD shall be thy confidence, and shall keep thy foot from being taken. Withhold not good from them to whom it is due, when it is in the power of thine hand to do it. Proverbs 3:23-27[KJV]

All the dreams I dreamed I am now able to understand the meaning with the exception of the dream from January 16, 2011. The journey thus far was not easy. Respectfully, understanding that pain produces the anointing, and God's glory shines bright. I stand firmly on the scripture below:

So shall my word be that goeth forth out of my mouth: it shall not return unto me void, but it shall accomplish that which I please, and it shall prosper in the thing whereto I sent it. [Isaiah 55:11 KJV]

Every beginning is attached to a journey, and an ending. The journey may be short-term or long-term. Nevertheless, I conclude with these words: Although people have a voice, and they mean well, and will speak well but Samuel nearly made a mistake in his judge when preparing to anoint the next appointed king. God spoke and prevented the mistake from happening. God spoke over Solomon's life, and Solomon responded accordingly, but one day Solomon lost his way hanging around with the wrong company.

LET ME SEE YOUR FEET

*W*aking up the dream on January 16, 2011, thinking about Roberts's request, saying, "Let me see your feet." I remembered how we both started laughing when I removed my house sock from my right foot exposing the red polish on my toe nails. I wiggled my toes and we both started laughing. I looked into his face to see him laughing, and I woke up. I knew he was standing in the exact spot where the right wing landed from the explosion of the jet [February 13, 2006 dream]. The scripture concerning Moses feet is resonating in my spirit:

And he said, Draw not nigh hither: put off thy shoes from off thy feet, for the place whereon thou standest is holy ground. Exodus 3:5 [KJV]

As Robert was parking his Cadillac on the shoulder of Stemmons Freeway, I watch him open his car door slowly. The first thing I saw was his feet. I watch as his fine designer shoes touched the ground. He walked like a king, and I watched each step he took. His legs were slightly bowed, and he was well coordinated to be so tall. His posture was that of authority. He was structured and everything about him was different from most gentlemen I met previously. Robert's disposition made a statement about him without spoken words. His inner spirit was complimenting the gentleman who was walking towards my direction. He was well-groomed, impeccably stylish with a fine taste in the fashion, well-versed, well-traveled, fit, slender, athletically fit, standing about six feet four inches tall. He was polished, distinctive, distinguished, preppy, and debonair. He wore expensive designer shoes.

Dear Robert, It is my prayer and desire for this book to reach you wherever the soul of your feet maybe. God knows where you are, and I know he is watching over you. The soul of your feet had touched foreign land, and I have always prayed for you. When I thought we were home with the LORD, the LORD would grant me a dream of a tall slender man, which reminded me of you. I pray blessings to your mind, soul, and body that God would do not but bless you abundantly above and beyond what you could ask or think. I petition the LORD to bless you victoriously beyond what he did before.

I want you to know that I never stopped thinking about you. I apologize for pondering the words spoken by the audible voice of God. Even so, today, I am wondering if you too heard the audible voice as you as well were driving on Stemmons Freeway. It's been stated repeatedly that God works in mysterious ways. . So many moments I thought of sharing with you what thus saith the LORD, but I pondered not knowing if you could handle the supernatural. I look forward to hearing fifteen years worth of conversation from you. Robert, you may consider writing and publishing a book.

I pray I have the opportunity to outline the chapters and enjoy the developing details of your life plus the fifteen years after we met. As I was looking forward to meeting your mother, and getting to know you better, you were deployed to Bosnia. Taking the time to get to know you better was the plan, but a military plan for deployment interrupted the plan. When duty calls to protect this country, I am not selfish because I enjoy the freedom of living in America.

One day, I hope to understand the true meaning and the reason after fifteen years, the LORD finally allowed me to hear your voice and see your face. The exact meaning of the dream being revealed is with God, in his time. So many male songbirds have visited my backyard after the dream on January 16, 2011. The Scarlet Tanager, Red Cardinals, thirty Garden Warblers, three Mountain Bluebirds, two Blue Jays, and hosts of Ring-billed Gulls [flew over my backyard].

In a particular dream, I was walking along the seashore with a tall slender gentleman. He was walking behind me as I was running in and out of the mini waves rushing in and out from the sea upon the seashore. Suddenly, he called my name, saying, "Linda," with his arms opened wide for me come to him. Well, I did. Rising up out of the dream, I wondered about the gentleman because I love beautiful seashore especially walking along the shore. I was walking along the seashore without my shoes, and my toe nails were polished with red toe nail polish.

One interesting thought, rest on the words spoken by Robert, saying, "**I DID THIS FOR YOU**," was mentioned to me in a dream of seeing someone I know appear inside my actual master bedroom closet. Perhaps I will be able to expound on the dream in my next book. He was dressed in the same clothing for three consecutive days and then Robert appeared in an isolated window wearing the same clothing saying, "I DID THIS FOR YOU."

A lady name Tammy, that lives in Irving, Texas shared a word with me in 2004, while we were dining at Chili's in Arlington, Texas, after attending a worship service inside of a home, which was also located in Arlington. Tammy spoke a word to me double from God concerning my husband. I expressed to her that I was in agreement. However, I never spoke about hearing the audible voice of God on the freeway, and meeting Robert, the military aviation combat pilot. It was the one thing I enjoyed pondering.

I wish I knew the meaning of your spoken words from the dream saying, "I DID THIS FOR YOU.

ABOUT THE AUTHOR

I am a born again believer filled with the Holy Ghost. I am confident that God is a Spirit. I am a full time adult student studying psychology. I currently reside in Dallas, Texas. My desire is to include the study of theology because I like knowing what I do not know since I have executed Matthew 6:33. It is my desire and pursuit to engage in a new career as a Certified Professional Life Coach. Most of my time is spent reading academically, which is why I equally study the Bible daily and extensively. My background includes Human Resources, Banking, and Electrical Energy. I have previously published three books, which are out of print [The Back Porch: A Grandmother's Love and Prayers. The Back Porch A Grandmother's Love and Prayers Revision. "When I Get Married"].

During my free time, I write manuscript. I am currently writing manuscript for my next publications' titled "The Parable of Secrets," "Knowledge [spoken to me in a dream to write]," and a healthy cookbook featuring "The Ph.D., which is to be dedicated to my pastor. " I have a strong passion for photography, soy candles, Waterford Crystal, setting exclusive formal dining room tables. If I decided to develop a business for fine table décor, it may be titled "The Creative Touch of Elegance." I am fascinated with personalized greeting cards, which may be under the umbrella of "The Creative Touch of Elegance."

I enjoy talking live on Blog Talk Radio under the show titled, "The Quintessential Picnic." As you may have read, I got involved with writing at age seven, and it evolved over the years with frequent journaling. The release from journaling I discovered is deeply therapeutic. Attending

Bible study under the leadership of my Pastor Dr. Ervin D. Seamster, Jr. is always enlightening. Recently, I have learned to appreciate cooking with fresh herbs. I enjoy exercising, physical fitness, and the preparation of healthy meals prepared with certified organic foods.

Likewise, I enjoy fine French Soaps that are natural, which Mango and Rose Pedal soap. I love gardening [vegetables, herbs, and flowers]. I believe and respect the sanctity of marriage between a man and a woman. I relax in a sacred sanctuary sabbatical, which is when I retreat to an outdoor picnic by the lake to study my Bible, journal, and enjoy the openness of nature. Spending quality time enjoying a metamorphosis tea time in the midst of live butterflies is sweet serenity. They fly with such grace and poise. Spending incredible time with family is essential and the support of family is concrete. If I had to choose a name for my pending Certified Professional Life Coach. Endeavor it may be "The Sanctity of Marriage."

Focused on the journey of Jesus from a little child and mindful of all the things he encountered and accomplished up to the point of his ascension [Matthew 28:18 All power is given unto me in heaven and in earth]. Likewise, we are endued with power and knowledge [Luke 24:49 & James 3:13] to empower others. What I learned early in life, which serves as the catalyst to study psychology with an intense thirst and hunger, and study the bible with the same intensity. I believe the spiritual journey combined with the natural journey set the stage for the early experience to explode into the knowledge of higher learning. Education is never complete until the brain is dead, meaning the absence of the breath of life. Education and knowledge are the first employment to gain.

I support our Military, Pastors/Ministers, Government Leaders, National Leaders, Education, and all the families of the world. I prefer the simple elegant life. Since learning the harm and danger of stress, I especially prefer and desire the simple elegant life. In conclusion, I am a prayer warrior, and I am ready to travel abroad.